THE ♛ CHESS KID'S ♟ BOOK

of the King and Pawn Endgame

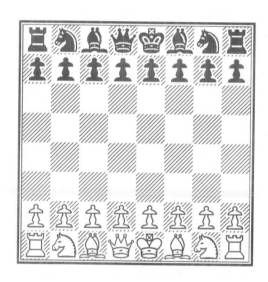

David MacEnulty

Random House
Puzzles & Games

Library of Congress Cataloging-in-Publication data is available.

0 9 8 7 6 5 4 3 2 1

ISBN: 0-8129-3510-1

New York   Toronto   London   Sydney   Auckland

Acknowledgments

I am very grateful to National Masters Mitchell Fitzko and Mike Klein for their thoughtful suggestions in the development of this manuscript.

I would also like to thank my students from C.E.S. 70 in the Bronx; in teaching them, I was forced to clarify many ideas, and find or develop exercises that were understandable and useful to children. They also taught me a lot about how smart children are. I will always be thankful for the opportunity I had to work with these wonderful kids.

Above all, I thank Bruce Pandolfini for introducing me to these ideas, and for his generous support and wise commentary as I worked on this book.

for Edward and Elizabeth

Contents

Introduction

"Most people play the endings badly." This truism was my major reason for wanting to learn to play the ending well. I figured that since most people play the ending badly, if a chess game came down to the ending and I knew what was happening and my opponent didn't, even if I had a slightly worse position, I might be able to turn the game around. And if I had a good position, I wanted to be sure I could turn my advantage into a win. I certainly didn't want a potential win to turn into a draw or a loss.

I had a good reason for this. Many years ago, I played a casual game with a Spanish master in Barcelona. I was feeling pretty good about the game, and I was amazed that I had gotten down to what I thought was an even position with just the Kings and a few Pawns. However, three moves after the last of the big pieces left the board, it was clear that I had no chance at all. The master had maneuvered me into an ending where, in spite of the material equality, I was dead lost. I had no ideas at all regarding the ending, and he was a wizard.

Many years later I met another wizard in the endgame, Bruce Pandolfini. He taught me some of the basic ideas, and pointed me in a direction that has resulted in this book.

When I began teaching chess to elementary school children, I realized that most students don't get much training in the endings. While it's true that many children's games end in checkmate before reaching the endgame, there are still a lot of games that come down to a King and Pawn ending.

If you play in tournaments, each win is vitally important to you and to your team. The knowledge you can gain from this book will lead to winning many more games than you would win otherwise. And if your opponent knows what is in this book and you don't, you will be at a big disadvantage in a King and Pawn ending.

The ideas and exercises in this book have been tried out by the chess team at the school where I taught in the Bronx.

By the second grade, many kids are ready to understand some of these ideas; by the third grade most are capable of even bigger leaps. The most proficient fourth and fifth graders could absorb everything in this book, and their games showed it. The ideas in this book are not easy, and some children may have more difficulty than others with this material. People develop at different rates. When a student has trouble learning some of this, I suggest waiting a few months or a year and trying again. There are plenty of other valuable chess concepts that can be learned in the meantime.

Since my students were well versed in such ideas as the Square of the Pawn, Opposition, Key Squares, the Outside Passed Pawn, and other basic concepts of the ending, we won an overwhelming majority of the games that came down to a King and Pawn ending.

The following ending is a dramatic example from one of our tournaments. This game was played in a National Elementary Scholastic Tournament. Fifth grader Naeem Holman played the Black pieces.

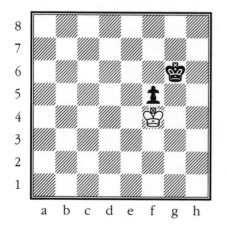

1.	Kf4-f3	Kg6-g5
2.	Kf3-g3	f5-f4 +
3.	Kg3-f3	Kg5-f5
4.	Kf3-f2	Kf5-g4
5.	Kf2-g2	f4-f3 +
6.	Kg2-f2	Kg4-f4
7.	Kf2-f1	Kf4-g3
8.	Kf1-e1??	(see diagram on next page)

This game should have been a dead draw. In fact, White played seven perfect moves, but then he made a huge goof on move eight.

Position after 8. Kf1-e1??

Up until now, White was doing all the right moves. He moved straight back until Black moved to the side of the Pawn, when he took the opposition by getting directly under the Black King, forcing the pawn to move forward with check. If he had just done that one more time—the time when it mattered the most—he would have gotten the draw. Fortunately for Naeem, his opponent either forgot the drawing method or he didn't know it, but in any case, his move to e1 allowed the crushing **9. Kg3-g2**, guarding the promotion square and guaranteeing a new Black Queen, and an easy win. Had White simply played 8. Kf1-g1, Naeem wouldn't have won.

Naeem knew his endings, and his opponent didn't, and that knowledge helped make his team the National Champions that year.

Another important reason for learning these endings is to avoid losing. As we just saw, Naeem's opponent could have avoided losing if he just knew what to do on that critical eighth move. But there is another point to this idea of not losing. *In many positions, playing for the win is not reasonable.* In trying for too much, a player can turn a solid draw into a terrible loss. Better to take home half a point for a draw than to bring a zero back for losing.

This position, for example, well known to chess theory, is not winning for White.

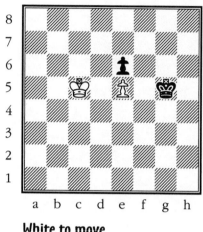

White to move.

Yet in a game, one of my students tried to win it, and ended up losing. (See page 75 for a full explanation of this position.)

There are millions of possible King and Pawn endings, and no book can possibly treat all of them. Instead we begin with fundamental positions where we know for sure what should happen, given best play by both sides.

From there, we branch out to more complex ideas, and little by little, we build a body of knowledge that leads us to become strong endgame players. Although there are millions of possible King and Pawn positions, many of them fall into categories where if you know the big idea of one position, you can then figure out the many positions similar to that one. For example, the Square of the Pawn is a big idea that governs thousands of particular situations, and the same is true of opposition, key squares, and all of the other themes in this book.

This book is all about the big ideas that govern King and Pawn endings. The wonderful fact is that those who know these big ideas play the ending well and win more games than those who don't.

c h a p t e r

1

Four Fundamental Positions and Two Big Ideas

when does the endgame start?

This is one of those fuzzy areas, but we can say there are certain essential ingredients for what chess players call the endgame.

First, most of the pieces and many of the Pawns are off the board, and the danger of an immediate checkmate is usually not present. Since the danger to the King is far less than in the earlier parts of the game, the Kings can—*and should*—come out to play. A cardinal principle of the ending is: **ACTIVATE THE KING!** One reason so many students play the ending badly is that they fail to use this very powerful piece.

Second, the essential idea of the ending frequently revolves around the question of who can promote a Pawn first. While there are many different kinds of endings—Rook endings, Bishop against Knight endings, Minor piece against Rook endings, Queen endings, Queen against minor pieces, etc.—as the great Paul Keres once wrote, most of these evolve into Pawn endings, making Pawn endings "the cornerstone of the whole of endgame theory."

Since the King is so important in these endings, I'd like to give you two new ways of thinking about the King.

1. **The king is a fighting piece.** Most people view the King as a slow weak piece that must be protected. In the point evaluation of the pieces, a Pawn is worth only one point, Bishops and Knights are worth approximately three points, Rooks are worth five points and the Queen gets a huge nine points. The poor King isn't even assigned any points. Many teachers say the King is worth the whole game, but that only addresses the King's importance. It doesn't tell us his strength relative to the other pieces. As fighting units, these points give us an idea of their fighting strength. So what is the King worth as a fighting unit? The general consensus is that the King is worth about four points. That makes it stronger than a Knight or a Bishop, but a little less than a Rook. With a piece that powerful, doesn't it make sense to send the King out to fight in the ending? In fact, that is a *requirement* of these endings.

2. **The king has a huge footprint.** Think about the King not as a slow piece that just moves one square at a time, but as a big block of nine squares, thumping his huge footprint down on every step.

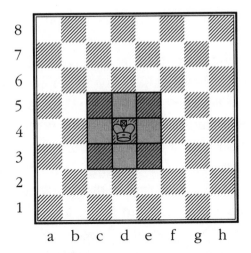

That's a big block of squares the King controls. Every time the King takes a step, that big block of squares moves. The King doesn't appear so weak anymore, does it?

The King is a powerful piece. In the endgame, you must use this monster with the big footprint.

One more **big** idea regarding the King: In many of these endings, you want to get your King to its most powerful position before advancing the Pawn. This big guy with the big footprint likes to get in front of his pawn to lead the way through danger.

Unless it's a race the Pawn can win—see Chapter Two: The Square of the Pawn—the friendly King wants to guard his fragile Pawn. Sending a Pawn out on its own is like sending a six-year old across town on his own. The little guy needs a big protector to help get him across the board.

Another really **big** idea in the ending is the draw.

A draw is a tie game in chess. Nobody wins and nobody loses. In a chess tournament, each game is worth one point, so if the game is a draw, the players split the point. Each player gets a half point.

There are six ways to draw. For a complete understanding of how to claim draws, players should consult the USCF *Official Rules of Chess*.

1. **Agreement:** both players simply agree to stop playing and split the point.

2. **Lack of checkmating material:** If both players only have a King left on the board, or if either side has only a Bishop or a Knight against a lone King, the game is a draw because no one can force checkmate. A variation of this in tournament play occurs when a player runs out of time on the clock, but the opponent does not have checkmating material. The game is a draw. Normally, you lose if you run out of time, but if your opponent can't win, then you can't lose. If your opponent doesn't have the pieces to inflict a checkmate, there is no way to win. Since nobody can win, the game is a draw.

3. **Threefold occurrence of position:** If a position occurs three times during the course of a game, the player about to create the third occurrence can ask for a draw. **Perpetual Check**, where one side can simply check the enemy King forever, ultimately will produce a threefold occurrence of position, so rather than play it out until a certain position has been reached three times, the players just call it a draw.

4. **Stalemate:** If the side to move is not in check and has no legal moves, the game is a draw by stalemate.

5. **Fifty move rule:** If fifty moves have passed with no piece being captured or no Pawn having moved, the game can be called a draw.

6. **Insufficient losing chances:** This one is a little tricky, and is usually claimed when one player is almost out of time but has a good position. The definition of no losing chances is that the position is such that a "C" player would not lose to a master, given unlimited time.

The draw in chess is very important, because if you are losing and can somehow force a draw, you get half a point, where you would have gotten nothing. If you are winning, and blunder into a draw, the full point you would have had for winning becomes only a half-point.

On the next pages we look at four fundamental positions. These positions are the basis for all king and pawn endings.

Practice and memorize these four positions.

Fundamental Position #1

Our first diagram shows one of the most important positions in king and pawn endings.

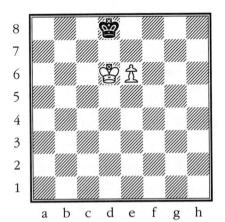

A Most Important Position

Nobody wants to move. Black to move loses; White to move draws. Naturally that means that if Black moves first, White wins!, and if White moves first, Black doesn't lose.

ZUGZWANG.

Zugzwang is a German word, meaning 'compulsion to move.'

This position demonstrates this vital idea in chess endings. In the opening or the middle of the game, one of the most important weapons a player can have is the right to make the next move.

In endings, there are positions where you *don't* want to move. Any move you make will be bad for you. However, in chess you cannot 'pass,' so the compulsion to move can sometimes hurt.

In the above diagram, neither side wants to move. If White moves first, he only gets a draw. If Black moves first, he loses. *When any move you make will create a worse position than you have, you are in* **zugzwang.**

Now let's see why neither side wants to move.

If Black moves first, we have:

| 1. | ... | Ke8 |
| 2. | e7 | Diagram |

White advanced the Pawn to the seventh rank *without giving check*.

Black would like to just stay on e8 in front of the Pawn. Unfortunately for Black, the King has only one possible move. You can't pass in chess, so,

2.	...	Kf7 the only move.
3.	Kd7	guarding the promotion square.
3.	...	K any
4.	e8=Q	wins.

So Black doesn't want to move first.

If White moves first, we have:

   1. e7+   *advance with check and your game is a wreck.*
   1. ...   Ke8
   2. Ke6 stalemate. Diagram

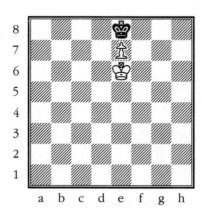

Any other White move allows Black to capture the Pawn, with a draw.

So White doesn't want to move first either.

In our starting position, Fundamental Position #1, both sides are in zugzwang, or what we call *mutual zugzwang*

By the way, that cute little ditty,

Advance with Check

And your game is a wreck

applies to positions where there are two Kings and one Pawn on the board, and the Pawn is advancing to the seventh rank. You don't want to advance to the seventh with check. In the ending mentioned in the introduction where White could have had the draw by playing his King to f1, that would have forced Naeem to advance with check. His game would then have been a wreck. The win becomes a draw.

At the beginning of this chapter, I suggested that you practice these fundamental positions. I would now like to pass on some wisdom every musician knows. Contrary to what you may have been told, practice does not make perfect. Practice makes permanent. It's perfect practice that makes perfect performance. If you practice poorly, you will play poorly. If you practice with precision, you will play with precision.

Fundamental Position #2

Our second fundamental position shows the importance of having your King in front of the pawn. Here, White did not do that, allowing the Black King to get in front of the pawn. Once Black has the King on the seventh rank directly in front of the advancing Pawn, the Pawn should not be able to promote. *It is still possible for Black to make a mistake; however, with best play this will always be a draw.*

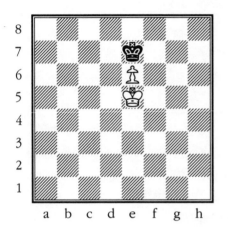

If the weak side's King can block the Pawn on the seventh rank, the game should be drawn, no matter where the White King is or who has the move.

Black draws as long as the King moves straight up and down between e7 and e8 until White's King moves to either d6 or f6.

When White's King moves to d6, the Black King moves to d8. When White's King moves to f6, the Black King moves to f8.

In this way, Black assures that whenever the Pawn moves to the seventh rank, it will advance with check and, as we saw in the previous example, White's game will be a wreck.

The important thing is for Black to wait until White commits to one side of the pawn, and *then* move to the same side.

Let's play this out.

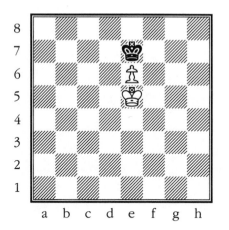

Possible moves:

1.	Kd5	Ke8
2.	Kd6	Kd8
3.	Ke5	Ke7
4.	Kf5	Ke8
5.	Kf6	Kf8
6.	Ke5	Ke7

White can make no progress as long as the Black King *waits* for the White King to go to one side or the other and then goes to the same side. Notice that all Black did was go straight up and down on the file the Pawn is on until White advanced his King to the sixth rank.

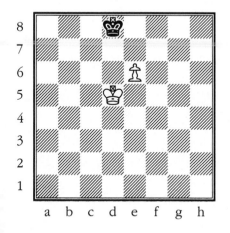

A mistake for Black would be to move to the side before White does.

1.	Kd5	Kd8?? Diagram
2.	Kd6!	Ke8
3.	e7	advancing the Pawn without check!
3.	...	Kf7
4.	Kd7	K any
5.	e8=Q winning.	

Equally bad would have been

1.	Kd5	Kf8??
2.	Kd6	Ke8
3.	e7	advancing without check!
3.	...	Kf7
4.	Kd7	K any
5.	e8=Q	winning.

Play this out several times until you are very familiar with the ideas behind these moves. The more you practice good moves, the better you will get.

Fundamental Position #3

The third fundamental position is called **Guarding the Path.** The idea is very simple. When all that is left are two Kings and a Pawn, if the strong side's King protects every square down to promotion, the opposing King is helpless. Here, the White King *guards the path* of the pawn down to promotion. If the Black King cannot capture the pawn on this move, White wins.

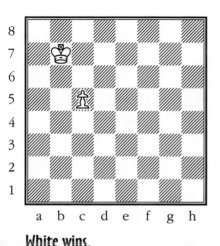

We left out the Black King in this diagram, because unless Black can capture the Pawn on the move, it doesn't matter where the Black King is.

White wins.

In this beautiful position, no matter what Black does, White's next three moves are:

1. c6
2. c7
3. c8=Q

This is one of the few times in chess when you don't care what your opponent does, because there are no moves that are dangerous. As long as Black cannot capture the Pawn on this move, Black's moves are of no concern.

Fundamental Position # 4

Here again, we have a clear win for White, and we don't care whose move it is or where the opposing King is. With best play, White wins.

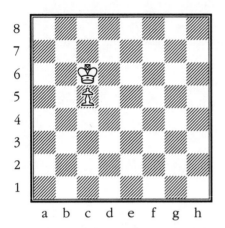

Win for White no matter where the Black King is or who has the move.

Again, we have left off the Black King, because White wins no matter where the Black King is.

In the bottom diagram we have added a Black King on c8.

With **Black to move**, the King would have to go to either b8 or d8. White then plays to the opposite side and guards the path with Kd7 or Kb7 as in **Fundamental Position #3.**

White to move also wins. White simply moves the King to either side (b6 or d6) and walks in with the Pawn.

1. Kd6   Kd8
2. c6   Kc8
3. c7   advancing without check!
3. ...   Kb7   only move.
4. Kd7   guarding the promotion square, and no matter what Black does, White plays
5. c8=Q   winning.

It would be a very good idea to play this out several times until you are completely familiar with the moves associated with this position.

In addition to the four fundamental positions, there are two more **big** ideas to keep in mind.

1. The Universe of the Pawn.

The Universe of the Pawn is the file the Pawn is on and the two files immediately beside that file.

When the Kings are fighting over the Pawn's survival, neither King wants to leave the Universe of the Pawn.

Beginners frequently go wandering off with their King, and they lose the Pawn as a result. In this position, a second grade student played

    1. Ke4?   (leaving the Universe of the Pawn), and Black quite happily jumped down with

    1. ...   Kc5, blocking the Pawn. White then made a bad situation even worse with

    2. Ke5??   And Black won the Pawn after

    2. ...   Kc4;

    3. Ke4   Kxc3   Black had the draw.

As we will see in the Chapter on the Opposition, White should have won this with ease.

On the next page, we have one more example of this idea of leaving the Universe of the Pawn.

The Universe of the Pawn

In this position, reached at a New York City Tournament between two second graders, White stepped out of the Universe. The girl playing Black immediately went after the lonesome White Pawn, and got a draw. The moves were:

1. Ka6??   Kc6

The Black King now blocks the White King from approaching the Pawn. Because the White King left the Universe, the Pawn is lost.

2. Ka5   Kc5
3. Ka4   Kc4
4. Ka3   Kxc3

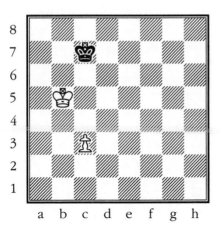

Once it left the Universe of the Pawn, the White King could do nothing to save the Pawn.

Had he played **1.** Kc5, staying in the Universe of the Pawn, White should win. When you have studied the chapters on Opposition, Out-flanking, and Key Squares, you should win this every time, even if you are playing the World Champion.

2. The second **big** idea is when the enemy King is near the Pawn, the friendly King wants to get in front of its Pawn and advance to its most powerful position before the Pawn advances.

You may have noticed that in Fundamental Positions One and Two, the friendly King was not in front of the Pawn. In the first fundamental position, White only wins if it is White to move. In the second, with the Black King in front of the Pawn, White only wins if Black makes a terrible mistake. Don't count on that happening.

In Fundamental Positions Three and Four, White wins every time because *the friendly King is in front of the Pawn.*

In this position, White usually won't advance the Pawn until the Black King has been pushed down to the eighth rank.

After you have done the chapters on the Opposition, Outflanking, and Key squares, come back and play this one out.

c h a p t e r

2

Square of the Pawn

What happens when a Pawn has a race with the enemy King down to the promotion square? Well, if the Pawn wins the race, it becomes a Queen, and that is usually enough to win the game. If the King wins the race, it's good-bye Pawn.

Assuming the friendly King is too far away to offer protection, how can we tell if the Pawn can beat the King?

Simple counting is one way. How many moves will it take the Pawn to reach the promotion square? How many moves will it take the opposing King to reach the promotion square? If they both get there in the same number of moves, the Pawn loses.

Let's look at an example. Here the White King is clearly not going to be any help. So how many moves will it take the Pawn to reach a8? Simple counting tells us it will get there in four moves.

Now, how many moves will it take the Black King to reach the same square? Again, simple counting tells us the answer is also four. So the King will catch the Pawn.

However, there is an easier way to figure this out. It's called the Square of the Pawn. To understand this a little better, let's review what a square is.

A square is a plane figure with four equal sides connected by four right angles.

Here we have a simple square.

How many squares is this?

If you answered four, you forgot something. The four smaller squares are inside a larger square, so the correct answer is actually **five**. (There are also four rectangles, but they don't concern us here.)

So now that we see that there can be squares within squares, let's look at the chessboard in a new way.

Every chess player knows there are sixty-four squares on the board. But with our new way of looking at squares, there are actually two hundred and four squares on the chessboard.

There are eight small squares in each rank, and there are eight ranks, so that gives us $8 \times 8 = 64$.

But if we join four squares together to make a larger square, like this,

then we have many more squares on the board. In fact, there are 49 such squares on the chessboard.

If we also look at the squares that are made up of nine smaller squares (3 by 3),

then we have 36 more squares.

Then there are twenty-five more that are made up of sixteen smaller squares (4 by 4). The first is from a1 to a4 to d4 to d1 and back to a1.

You can see that if we keep going this way, we end up with:

64 small squares

49 squares 2 by 2 (a1-a2-b2-b1-a1 is the first)

36 squares 3 by 3 (a1-a3-c3-c1-a1 is the first)

25 squares 4 by 4 (a1-a4-d4-d1-a1 is the first)

16 squares 5 by 5 (a1-a5-e5-e1-a1 is the first)

9 squares 6 by 6 (a1-a6-f6-f1-a1 is the first)

4 squares 7 by 7 (a1-a7-h7-h1-a1 is the first)

1 square 8 by 8 (a1-a8-h8-h1-a1)

---

204 total squares on the chessboard

Now that we can view the squares on a chessboard in this new way, let's go back to the Square of the Pawn.

To find the Square of the Pawn, we want to find one of the squares we were just discussing, where one corner is where the Pawn starts. All we do now is make a square out in the direction of the enemy King.

Let's start with the first position we were examining in this chapter.

The Pawn is on a4. If we make a square down to the bottom of the board where one side is from a4 to a8, there are five squares on that side. That means each side of our large square will be made of five smaller squares. So this square runs from a4 to a8, from a8 to e8, from e8 back up to e4, and then across to a4.

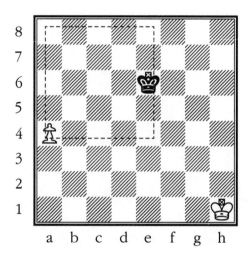

Why is this important? Because the Square of the Pawn is the danger zone. If the opposing King can get in that square, the Pawn is in danger. The King can catch the Pawn.

We don't have to actually count out the number of moves. We can just make a square down to the end of the board, with the Pawn as our starting point.

And now it's time for another clever trick. We don't even have to count out the squares!

The easiest and most reliable way to quickly see if the enemy King is in the square is to start with the Pawn, make a diagonal down to the bottom of the board on the side the enemy King is on, come back up the file to the rank the Pawn is on, and back to the Pawn again.

If the King is inside our imaginary line, or if it can get inside the line on his move, the Pawn can be caught.

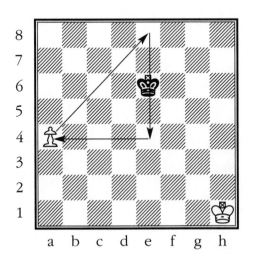

If the Black King had been on c3, d3, e3 or anywhere on the f-file from f3 to f8, with Black to move, the King could still catch the Pawn on any of those squares. Any move toward the Pawn will put the Black King in the square of the Pawn. Of course, if the Black King had been on a3 or b3 with Black to move, it would simply take the pawn immediately. However, if it had been White to move, the Pawn, moving to a5, would be safe.

On the next page, we show a very important addition to this rule.

Square of the Pawn

The Square of the Pawn is one of the fundamental ideas in many king and pawn endings. If the enemy king can get inside the square, it will catch the pawn.

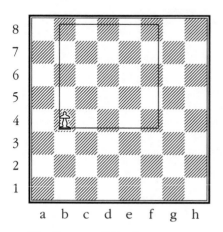

The Square of the Pawn.

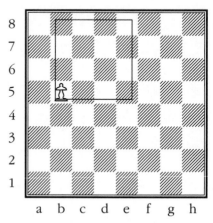

As the Pawn moves up, the square gets smaller . . .

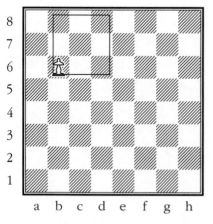

and smaller . . .

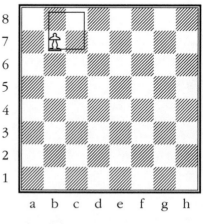

and smaller . . .

Using the Square of the Pawn

(answers on p. 110)

1. Is the Black King in the square?

2. What happens if
   1) White to move?
   2) Black to move?

3. White to move. Is the Black King in the Square? Careful, there is a trick to this one.

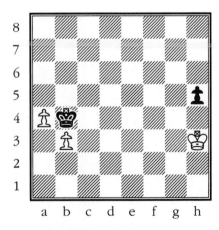

4. Can White win?

Two more big Ideas About the Square of the Pawn

1. Guard from Behind

As we saw in the last diagram on the previous page, the Black King could not capture the Pawn on b3 that was protecting the Pawn on a4. If it did, it would be behind the a4-Pawn. That would put it outside the square, and it would be White's move.

The Pawn would move forward, out of reach. The King would move up behind it again, and the Pawn would move out of reach again. They would repeat this useless chase until the Pawn promoted to a Queen.

That gives us the important idea that if the Square of the Pawn is the issue, a Pawn can be safely protected from behind.

In the diagram below, Black can save his Pawn by simply playing the Knight to d5. If White takes the Knight, the King will be outside the square of the Pawn.

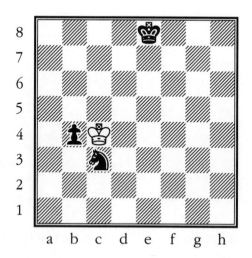

1.	...	Nd5
2.	Kxd5	b3
3.	Kc4	b2
4.	Kc3	b1=Q and wins.

2. Block the Path

In this diagram, although it is White to move, and White has two Pawns to Black's one, Black feels confident of the draw, and may even be thinking about winning. After all, the Black King is very close to the Pawns, and the Black Pawn is a threat to both White Pawns.

White's next move ruins those thoughts. What does White do?

White blocks the path of the King.

1.	f6!	Black has to capture, or the f-Pawn marches down.
1.	...	gxf6
2.	h5	Ke5
3.	h6	Kf5 The direct path is blocked, so the King must take a detour, and that takes too much time.
4.	h7	Kg6
5.	h8=Q	and an easy win.

These two tricks, guarding a Pawn from behind, and blocking the path of the King, are good to remember when the Square of the Pawn is the main feature of the position.

On the next few pages, we will show two other big ideas that are based on the Square of the Pawn: Two Pawns Separated by a Single File, and the Moving Square.

Two Pawns Separated by a Single File

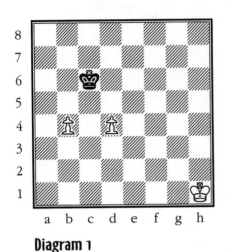

Diagram 1

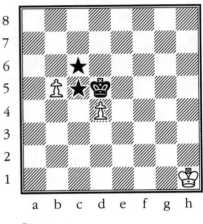

Diagram 2

When two Pawns are separated by a single file, they can protect each other by well-timed advances. If it is White to move, there is a problem right away. Moving either Pawn allows Black to take that Pawn and be in the square of the other one. Since moving either Pawn loses, White brings his king closer: **1. Kg2.**

If it is Black to move:

1. ...   Kd5   Black attacks one of the Pawns.

2. b5!   See the second diagram. Now there is a barrier (shown by the two stars) that the Black King cannot cross. The squares c5 and c6 are both guarded by the Pawns. (If **1. ... Kb5; 2. d5** is similar.)

If Black takes the d4-Pawn, the King will be out of the square of the b5-Pawn, and the Pawn will simply race down to promotion. Black has little choice.

2. ...   Kd6

Now if White plays **3. d5?**, Black takes the Pawn and is in the square of the other one. White will lose both pawns. Pushing the b5-Pawn also throws away the win (work this out on your own).

Two Pawns Separated by a Single File

Since moving either Pawn is bad, White brings the King up.

3. Kg2   Kc7

Now that the Black King cannot take the advancing d-Pawn, it is time to level the Pawns. Leveling the Pawns means to bring them to the same rank.

4. d5   Kb6
5. d6   (Diagram)   and the dance begins again.

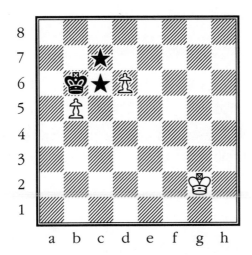

Once again, White builds a wall between the Pawns.

And once again, if Black takes one Pawn, the other one runs safely to promotion.

Black must once again retreat:

5. ...   Kb7

Again, it is not safe to advance either Pawn, so:

6. Kf3   Kc8

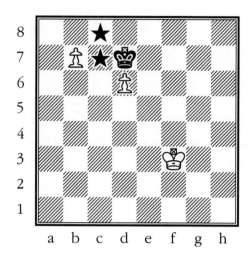

Now it is safe to again level the Pawns:

7. b6!   Kd7   (or ... Kb7; **8.** d7!)
8. b7!   Diagram

Black is helpless. The wall is up once more, and this time it is fatal. The b-Pawn will promote.

Dangerous Moments

- ◆ Do not level the Pawns if the King can capture one immediately. The King simply takes the Pawn, is still in the square of the other one. Wait for the King to retreat before leveling the Pawns.

- ◆ Do not push the forward Pawn two squares ahead of the rear Pawn. The King will catch it and still be in the square of the other Pawn (see note to Black's move 2).

The Moving Square

When the distance across the Pawns is equal to the distance to the end of the board, they form a square that reaches the last rank. Unless the enemy King can take one of the Pawns on the move, the Pawns are safe.

When the Pawns form a square that reaches the last rank, they can beat the enemy King, even if it is inside the square.

Naturally, this won't work if the King can just take one of the Pawns immediately. For example, if the King were on g4 with Black to move, Black simply plays Kxh5 and it is in the square of the e-Pawn.

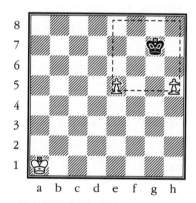

White wins no matter who moves.

Counting the files the Pawns are on, the distance across the Pawns is four files. Since they are also four ranks from the end, White wins.

1. ...   Kh6
2. e6   and Black is helpless. Taking on h5 leaves the King out of the square of the e-Pawn. If Black runs back to try to stop the e-Pawn with
2. ...   Kg7

then every White move wins. For example,

3. h6+   and now the King can do no more than choose which Pawn he will allow to promote.

3. ...	Kxh6	or	3. ...	Kf6
4. e7	Kg7		4. e7	Kxe7
5. e8=Q			5. h7	Kf7
			6. h8=Q	

The Moving Square

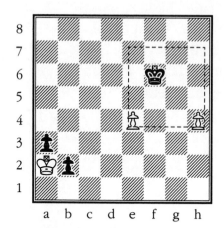

This time the square does not reach the last rank. The White Pawns are not safe.

Black to move and win
(Black also wins if it is White to move).

Black wins. In this diagram the Pawns are four files apart (remember, for this idea, we count the files the Pawns are on), but five squares from promotion. With the Black King in front and the White King tied down holding back the Black Pawns on a3 and b2, the White Pawns are not going to survive.

Notice that the White King cannot take the a3-Pawn, because it will then be outside of the square of the b2-Pawn: **1.** Kxa3, b1=Q and wins.

1.	...	Ke5
2.	h5	Kf6 (**2.** ... Kxe4 loses. The Black King will be outside the square of the h-Pawn, which simply marches down to promotion.)

If

3.	e5+	Kxe5 and the Black King is in the square of the h-Pawn.

If instead,

3.	h6	Kg6
4.	e5	Kxh6 and the Black King is in the square of the e-Pawn.

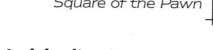
Practical Applications

Knowing the idea of the moving square is only useful if you can actually apply the idea to real situations in your games. In the position below, can you see how White can win by using the idea of the moving square?

The first step is to notice that the Pawns on e5 and h5 form a square down to the end of the board. They are four files apart (remember, we count the squares the Pawns are on for this) and four ranks from the bottom of the board. The trick is to get rid of the pesky Black Pawn on g7 that can stop the h-Pawn.

The winning method is **1. f6+!**, sacrificing the f-Pawn. **1. ... gxf6**, and now, not **2. exf6**, which lets Black take back with the King and he is in the square of the h-Pawn, but instead, 2. h6! Black has to go after the h-Pawn with **2. ... Kf7**. White now wins with **3. e6+** and Black has an impossible task. Take the e-Pawn, and the h-Pawn promotes. Go after the h-Pawn, and the e-Pawn promotes.

The moving square was too much for the Black King.

By the way, White could also have won with **3. h7, Kg7; 4. e6!**, and the Black King cannot take the h-Pawn and still get back to catch the e-Pawn, and it can't go after the e-Pawn without allowing the h-Pawn to promote.

Practical Applications

This famous position is from a game, Stoltz-Nimzovich. Can you find the Moving Square in this position? Using the same idea as in the previous example, can you find the winning idea for Black?

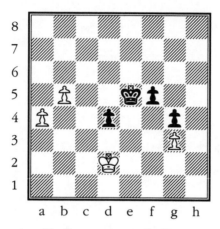

1. Black to move and win.

Here are two more puzzles to challenge you.

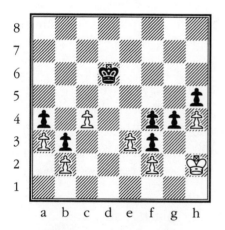

2. White to move and draw.

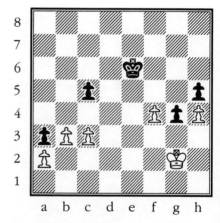

3. White to move and win.

The Opposition

Opposition is all about one King stopping the other King from making progress or one King pushing the other aside. In the diagram on the next page, neither King can move forward. If it is White to move, and the White King wants to get to d8, e8, or f8, the Black King can easily stop it. In fact, Black can stop the White King from even reaching the fifth rank.

White obviously cannot move up the board to d5, e5, or f5 at the moment. If the White King moves to f4, hoping to get to g5, Black simply steps in front by moving to f6. Once again, forward progress is impossible. Naturally, the same would be true if White tried to go to the other side: **1.** Kd4 is met by **1. ...** Kd6. Black can keep this up all day. When White moves to the side, Black just stays right with him, blocking all forward movement.

Now let's make it Black to move. Suddenly, the situation is completely different. The Black King must give up at least one of the squares in front of the White King. If Black moves to f6, that gives up the attack on d5. White can move forward by going to d5.

From this we can see that this is one of those peculiar situations in chess when you don't want to be the one to move. If White moves in the above diagram, he can make no progress. Black will *oppose* every move he makes. That is why, if it is White to move, we say that *Black has the opposition.* The side moving second can *block* whoever moves first.

However, if it is Black to move, then *White has the opposition.*

The Opposition

Opposition is a tool we use to push the enemy King out of the way. It is not a goal in and of itself. Opposition can be direct, distant, diagonal, or rectangular.

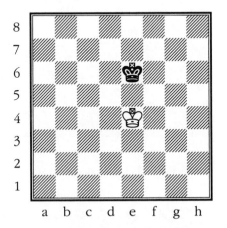

Direct Opposition: the Kings are one square apart on the same file.

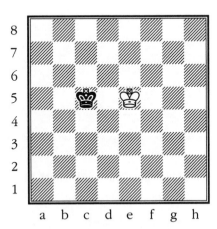

Or, as in this diagram, the same rank.

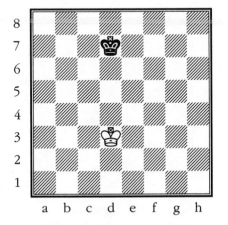

Distant Opposition: the Kings are on the same color square on the same rank or file.

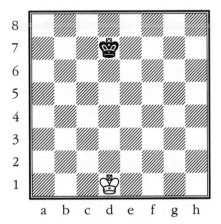

This is another example of distant opposition. Notice there is an *odd number* of squares between the Kings.

The Opposition

Diagonal Opposition: same diagonal, an odd number of squares apart.

Distant Diagonal Opposition: the Kings are on the same diagonal *an odd number of squares apart.*

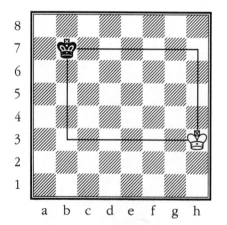

Rectangular Opposition: all four corner squares are the same color.

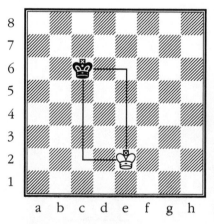

Rectangular Opposition: all four corner squares are the same color.

The Opposition

These different forms of opposition, distant, diagonal, rectangular, and others we haven't even mentioned, are valuable because, given a few moves, you can force your opponent into the direct opposition.

In the diagram above, for example, if White has the opposition, then it is, by definition, Black to move. How can White turn this into direct opposition? Let's look at some possible variations.

1.	...	Kd6
2.	Kd4	and White has it.

1.	...	Kc5
2.	Ke5	and White has it again, this time in a lateral position.

1.	...	Kc7
2.	Ke5	Kc8
3.	Ke6	Kd8
4.	Kd6	got it again.

if

3.	...	Kb8
4.	Kd6	Ka8
5.	Kc6	Kb8
6.	Kb6	and White has the direct opposition yet again.

Opposition Exercises

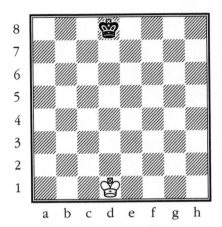

1. White to move and take the opposition.

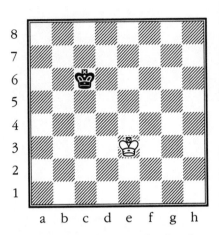

2. Black to move and take the opposition.

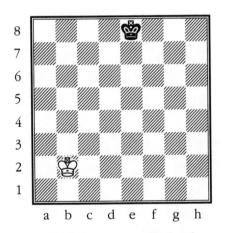

3. Black to move and take the opposition.

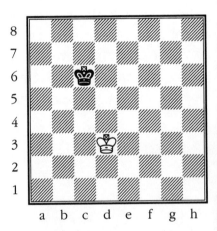

4. White to move and take the opposition.

Opposition

We said earlier that opposition is a tool one King uses to drive the enemy King out of the way. In this position, White obviously wants to promote the Pawn on f3, and Black wants to stop this from happening. In other words, the two Kings are in a battle to see which can get its way.

White to Move

Position after 4. Kc4.

Since it is White to move, White has a chance to seize the opposition.

1. Kf4! White takes the direct opposition.
1. ... Ke6
2. Ke4 Kd6
3. Kd4 Kc6
4. Kc4 It may seem strange that the White King gets in the way of the Pawn he wants to advance, but as we will see, this is frequently right where the King wants to be.

Now the Black King has to let the White King move up the board.

4. ... Kd6
5. Kb4! White uses the opposition to push the enemy King out of the way. When the Black King gives up the protection of one of the squares in front of the White King, White immediately grabs that square. In this case, Black gave up b5, so White hops to that square right away. This maneuver is called *Outflanking*, and we will learn more about it in the next chapter.

Opposition

Let's look at this position again. We mentioned in Chapter One that the friendly King wants to get in front of the Pawn and advance to its most powerful position before the Pawn advances. And we saw in Chapter Two, the Square of the Pawn, that without the protection of the friendly King, the Pawn can often be captured.

This is a perfect example of these two ideas. If the Pawn simply marches forward, it marches to its doom. The enemy King is in the square, and will quickly overtake the helpless Pawn.

Now it's time to introduce another **big** idea in King and Pawn endings: **the most direct route is often the wrong route.**

If White tries to get in front of the Pawn the most direct way, starting with Ke4, Black moves to e6, taking the opposition, and the Pawn will not promote.

Wrong would be:

1.	Ke4	Ke6!	And Black has the opposition.
2.	Kd4	Kd6	keeping the opposition.
3.	Kc4	Kc6	keeping the opposition.
4.	Kb4	Kb6	keeping the opposition.

5.	c4	Kc6 White can't get the opposition; his Pawn is on the square the King needs.
6.	c5	Kc7 moving straight back, so it can take the opposition again when the White King advances.
7.	Kb5	Kb7 taking the opposition again.
8.	c6+	Kc7 reaching **Fundamental Position #2** with a draw.
9.	Kc5	Kc8 moving straight back again to take the opposition no matter which way the White King advances.
10.	Kb6	Kb8 and we have **Fundamental Position #1** with White to move. Remember, in this position, *nobody wants the move.*
11.	c7+	White advances with check and his game is a wreck after
11.	...	Kc8
12.	Kc6	Stalemate.

Opposition

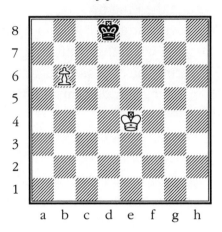

This position is another standard opposition exercise. In this case, White allows Black to take the opposition, knowing it cannot be held.

1. Kd5   Kd7   taking the opposition.
2. Kc5   and the White Pawn attacks the opposition square c7, so Black cannot maintain the opposition.

However, Black does have a clever trick to play.

2. ...   Kd8!
3. Kd6!   taking the opposition. White doesn't fall for the trick. Moving to c6, the most direct route, is the wrong way to go. See the next page.
3. ...   Kc8
4. Kc6   Kb8
5. b7   advancing without check!
5. ...   Ka7   the only move.
6. Kc7   guarding the promotion square.
6. ...   Ka6
7. b8=Q   and now, just for the fun of it, let's finish this off in two moves:
7. ...   Ka5
8. Qb3   Ka6
9. Qb6#

Let's look at what happens if Black plays the normal move:

2.   ...   Kc8
3. Kc6   Kb8   and White wins as in the main line.

Now let's start again and see what happens if White falls for Black's clever trick on move two.

1. Kd5   Kd7
2. Kc5   and the White Pawn attacks the opposition square, so Black cannot maintain the opposition.

However, Black does have a clever trick to play.

2.   ...   Kd8!
3. Kc6?   Kc8!   Black now has the opposition, and we have **Fundamental Position #1**, favoring Black. The Pawn will advance to the seventh rank with check, and Black will get the draw.

Opposition

In our last example, we saw that one side couldn't keep the opposition. The stronger side simply made a move that made it impossible for the weaker side to hold the opposition. This next puzzle is another example of that same idea.

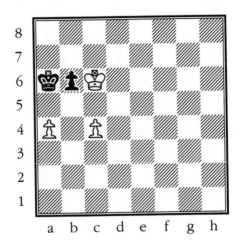

White can't advance either Pawn without losing them both. If **1. a5**, the Black King takes it and still protects its Pawn on b6. If **1. c5**, then **1. ... bxc5** removes the c-Pawn, and the Black King can easily take the a-Pawn in two moves.

1. Kc7 is answered by **1. ... Ka7**, keeping the opposition, and White gets nowhere.

The solution is to make a move that won't allow Black to keep the opposition. Since two pieces are not allowed to occupy the same space, White plays

 1. Kd6! Black can't play **1. ... Kb6**, because his own Pawn is in the way. And Black can't take the distant opposition, because the King is on the edge of the board. No matter what Black plays, White gets the opposition.

 1. ...   Kb7
 2. Kd7   Ka7

3. Kc7   Ka6

4. Kb8   and again, Black can't get the opposition because of his own Pawn. At first it may seem odd for the White King to deliberately go so far from the White Pawns. However, strangely enough, now every Black move loses. For example,

4. ...   Ka5

5. Kb7   Kxa4

6. Kxb6   Kb4

7. c5   and wins.

Play around with this position on your own. There are many interesting things to be learned here.

Opposition Exercises

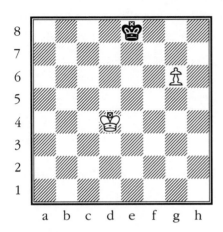

5. White to move and win. Yes, this is a mirror image of the example we gave earlier.

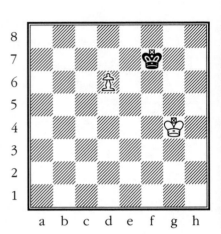

6. White to move and win. Again, Black has a way to get tricky.

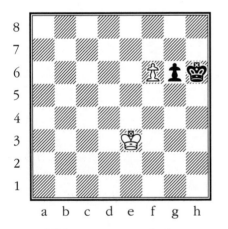

7. White to move and win.

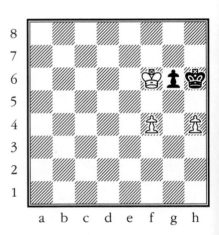

8. White to move and win.

Opposition Exercises

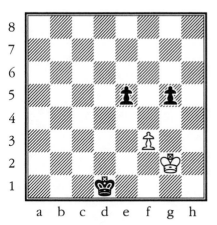

9. White to move and draw.

10. Black to move and draw.

11. White to move and win.

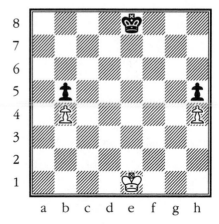

12. White to move and win.

c h a p t e r

4

Outflanking

The purpose of outflanking is to push the enemy king back. Outflanking and opposition work hand in hand.

As we saw in the previous chapter, when two Kings are in direct opposition, one King won't let the other pass. However, if one King is forced to move aside, that gives up a square that will allow the other King to make forward progress.

Since you can't go through the other King, you have to go around it. That maneuver is called *outflanking*. A *flank* is a side, so in outflanking, you attack from the side.

This position shows a typical outflanking maneuver. The purpose of this exercise is for the White King to get to one of the starred squares.

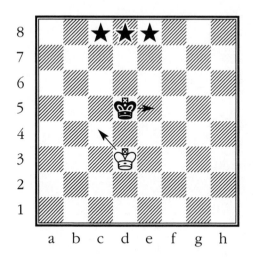

1. ...   Ke5   giving up control of c4.
2. Kc4!   White makes progress by outflanking. That is to say, White goes forward on the side of the Black King, and heads up the board.

White could also have played **2.** Ke3, keeping the opposition, *but that wouldn't make any forward progress. Opposition is not a goal in and of itself.* It is a technique for improving your king.

After **2.** Kc4, Black could take the diagonal opposition, **2.** ... Ke6, or the direct (laterally) with Ke4, but neither of these would stop White from just running straight down to c8. If the opposition won't stop your opponent, it isn't much good.

Outflanking

Let's follow this out to the end.

1.	...	Kd6
2.	Kd4	Opposition
2.	...	Kc6
3.	Ke5	Outflanking again
3.	...	Kd7
4.	Kd5	Opposition
4.	...	Ke7
5.	Kc6	Outflanking
5.	...	Kd8
6.	Kd6	Opposition
6.	...	Kc8
7.	Ke7	(Diagram) White will get to e8 with ease.

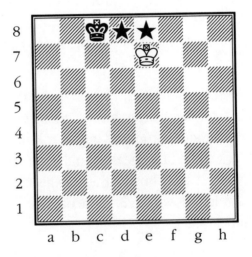

Outflanking and Opposition

We saw earlier that in this position, White could use the opposition to drive the enemy King out of the way. We left off with White holding the opposition in front of the Pawn, and Black having to give up control of one of the squares that would let the White King advance. We now know that maneuver is called *outflanking*. With this new technique, let's combine *opposition* with *outflanking,* and promote the Pawn.

We'll begin at the beginning. Both Kings are outside the Universe of the Pawn—in this case, the b, c and d files—and the Black King is in the square of the Pawn.

1.	Kf4!	White takes the direct opposition and holds it until his King is in front of the Pawn.
1.	...	Ke6
2.	Ke4	Kd6
3.	Kd4	Kc6
4.	Kc4	(Second diagram) Now the White King is in the center of the Universe of the Pawn.
4.	...	Kd6
5.	Kb5!	Outflanking
5.	...	Kc7
6.	Kc5	Opposition
6.	...	Kb7
7.	Kd6	Outflanking
7.	...	Kc8 (if **7.** ... Kb6, then **8.** c4! and the Pawn protects itself from a further advance of the Black King.)

Outflanking and Opposition

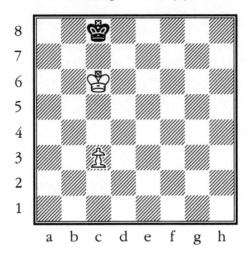

8. Kc6   Opposition (Diagram)

White has achieved the most powerful position for his King. Now the Pawn will simply march up to achieve **Fundamental Position #4**, which is a clear win for White.

8.	...	Kd8
9.	c4	Kc8
10.	c5	White has achieved **Fundamental Position #4**.
10.	...	Kb8
11.	Kd7	guarding the Path.
11.	...	Kb7
12.	c6+	K any
13.	c7	K any
14.	c8=Q	

Key Squares

Key Squares (sometimes called Critical Squares) are the squares your King must occupy to ensure the safe passage of the Pawn to the end of the board.

Black fights for the draw by keeping the White King off the key squares.

To find the key squares, just go up two ranks from the pawn. The key squares are the three squares right across the Universe of the Pawn.

The purpose of going up two ranks is to leave a space between the King and the Pawn. As you will see, that empty square between the pawn and the key squares is very important. With that empty square, you can gain the opposition if you don't already have it. So if you have a key square, you can win, *with or without the opposition.*

As you will see, we use opposition to get key squares, and then we use opposition and outflanking to keep them.

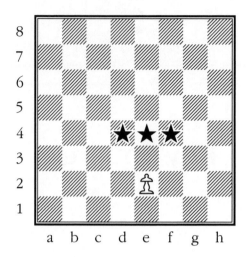

Once you have your King on a Key Square, if the only pieces on the board are the two Kings and your Pawn, even the World Champion can't keep you from winning the game.

Key Squares

Let's take a closer look at this important idea, following a Pawn as it moves up the board.

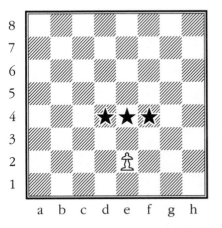
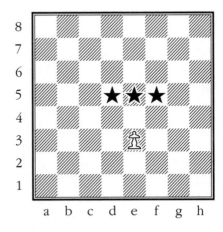

As the Pawn moves up the board, so do the Key Squares.

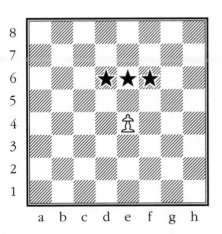
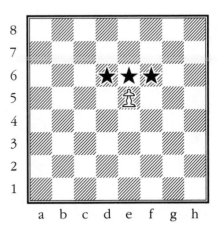

Once the Pawn crosses the middle of the board, you no longer need the spare Pawn move (see p. 59), and you get twice as many key squares.

In our fourth diagram, the Pawn has crossed the middle rank and has six key squares.

You might call these six squares Key Squares, but by the time you get down there you are in a more obvious battle with the opposing King to guard the promotion square and protect your Pawn. At this point, opposition and guarding the promotion square are far more important than key squares.

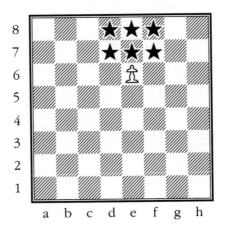

White wins if the White King can occupy any of the starred squares, always assuming the Black King cannot take the Pawn on the move.

In this diagram, the White King is on a Key Square for the Pawn on the fifth rank. You may recognize this as **Fundamental Position #4** from Chapter One. Let's review why White wins in this position, no matter whose move it is or where the Black King is.

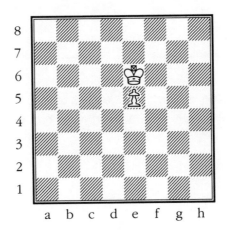

We'll put the Black King in its strongest position, right in front of the Pawn.

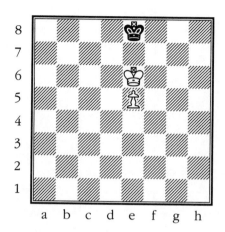

Black to move is easy.

1. ...   Kd8
2. Kf7,   guarding the path, and the Pawn simply marches in.
   If **1**. ... Kf8, then **2**. Kd7 accomplishes the same thing on the other side of the Pawn.

White to move is also an easy win.

1. Kd6   Kd8
2. e6   Ke8
3. e7   advancing without giving check.
3. ...   Kf7   The only move.
4. Kd7   Guarding the promotion square.
4. ...   K any
5. e8=Q   and wins easily.

Key Square Exercises

Name the key squares in each diagram.

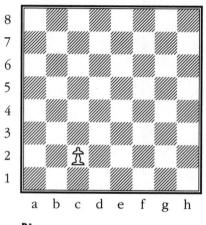

Diagram 1

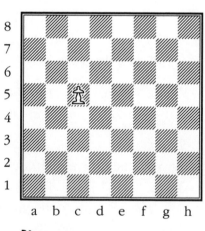

Diagram 2

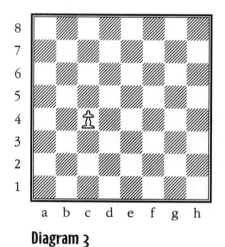

Diagram 3

Diagram 4

Key Squares

Let's look at the way to play the position when you have a key square already.

Black to Move

1. ... Kd6
2. Kb5 outflanking and White wins as before.

White to Move

There is a bit of a problem. With White to move, Black has the opposition. White can't make any progress with the King. But now we see the reason for that empty square between the Kings.

1. c3! Taking the opposition away from Black.
1. ... Kb6 giving up control of d5.
2. Kd5 Black gave it up, so White takes it.
2. ... Kc7

We have reached a position where people who don't know about key squares often make a mistake. If White pushes the Pawn to c4, that throws the key squares up to the sixth rank, and hands Black the opposition. White will not be able to get a key square, and the Pawn will not promote unless Black also makes a mistake. We can't blunder and then expect to have our opponent return the favor. Black plays the King to d7, taking the opposition, and White has no spare Pawn moves to get it back.

Remember, advance the King to its most powerful position before advancing the Pawn. *Black draws if he can keep White from getting a key square. The fight is not over the Pawn. The fight is over the key squares.*

3. Kc5   taking the opposition again.

3. ...   Kd7

Key Squares

Here again, White has a chance to make a mistake. **4.** c4 would again ruin the win. That just hands Black the opposition and with that Black can keep White from the key squares.

Diagram 1

4. Kb6   (Diagram 1) outflanking. White occupies a key square for the Pawn all the way up to c5.

A possible continuation might be:

4. ...   Kd8   (If **4.** ... Kc8, then **5.** Kc6 taking the opposition and the King position for the winning **Fundamental Position #4.**)

5. Kc6   and White is happy.

5. ...   Kc8

6. c4   Kd8

7. Kb7   guarding the Path and the Pawn walks into promotion no matter what Black does.

Now let's see how Black can get the draw if White plays **4.** c4.

Diagram 2

4.	c4	Kc7	taking the opposition and denying White the important key squares
5.	Kb5	Kb7	
6.	c5	Kc7	
7.	c6	Kc8	
8.	Kb6	Kb8	
9.	c7+	Kc8	
10.	Kc6	stalemate	

Key Square Exercises

White to move and win in all diagrams. Find the best move. As you will see, the key squares and the opposition are used together frequently. *The opposition is often the tool that gives you a key square.*

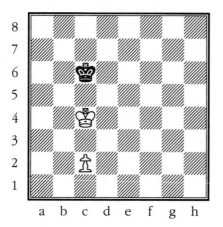

Diagram 5 (We just did this one on the previous page. Set it up on a board and see if you can do it.)

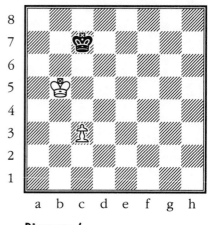

Diagram 6

Diagram 7

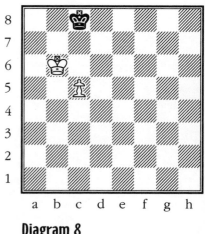

Diagram 8

Key Square Exercises

White to move and win in all diagrams. Step one is to identify the key squares. Step two is to find a path for the White King to get to a key square before the Black King can block him.

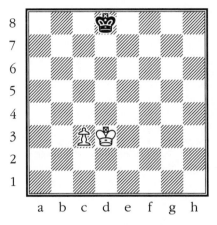

9. White to move and win.

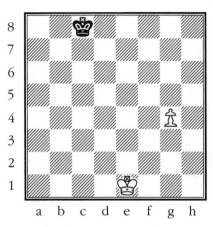

10. White to move and win.

11. White to move and win.

12. White to move and win.

Key Squares: Rook Pawns (a- and h-Pawns)

Preliminary Considerations. Rook Pawns are different from other Pawns. There are unique features to attacking and defending the Rook Pawns, because you can only come at them from one side.

If the enemy King can get in the corner, a lone King and a Rook Pawn cannot drive it out. The game will end in a draw. For example:

1. a7   stalemate.

Or

1. Kc7   Ka7
2. Kc6   Kxa6 draw.

Finally,

1. Kb5   Ka7
2. Ka5   Ka8
3. Kb6   Kb8
4. a7+   Ka8
5. Ka6   stalemate.

True, White could have fooled around a little more, but Black can easily hang out on a8, b8, or a7 forever (of course the draw by triple occurrence of position will settle things long before that).

Key Squares: Rook Pawns (a- and h-Pawns)

We just saw that, against a lone Rook Pawn, if the enemy King can hide out in the corner, the game will be a draw. What happens if the friendly King is imprisoned in the corner?

This has the same result. The game will be a draw. If the friendly King gets caught in the corner on a8, the enemy King can keep it there by occupying either c8 or c7. **1.** a7, Kc7 stalemate. Or **1.** Ka7, Kc7; **2.** Ka8, Kc8, etc. Obviously, similar situations arise in the other three corners as well.

When battling a lone Rook Pawn, the enemy King wants to either get in the corner himself, or lock the opposing King in the corner by occupying c8 (or f8 if it is a White h-Pawn, or c1 or f1 if White is battling a Black Rook Pawn).

Key Squares: Rook Pawns (a- and h-Pawns)

With these considerations in mind, Key squares for a Rook Pawn are on the seventh and eighth rank on the adjacent file. For White, the key squares are b7 and b8 for the a-Pawn, and g7 and g8 for the h-Pawn; for Black the key squares are b1 and b2 for the a-Pawn, and g1 and g2 for the h-Pawn.

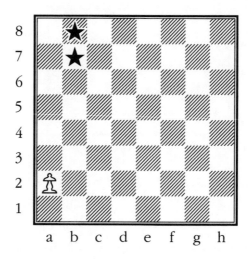

Once the White King occupies either b7 or b8, the Black King cannot get to the corner for the draw, nor can the White King be pushed into the corner for a draw.

Assuming the Pawn has safe passage down to a6, White has a guaranteed win once the King occupies the key squares.

The Defensive Key Square

As we mentioned earlier, if Black can keep the White King from occupying the key squares, the game should be a draw.

Against the a-Pawn, the Defender wants to occupy c8, since that keeps white from getting his key squares on b7 or b8.

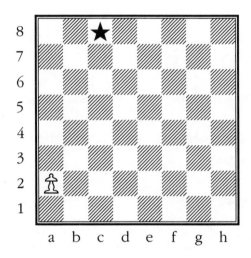

Similar considerations apply to the other three corners of the board.

Naturally, the defender would like to stop the Pawn earlier, and there are many ways to do that, but c8 is the last chance.

The only time occupying c8 won't work is if the Pawn has already advanced to a6 or a7 and the White King is on b6. A Black King arriving at c8 is too late to stop the Pawn from completing its march to promotion.

Key Squares: Rook Pawns (a- and h-Pawns) Exercises

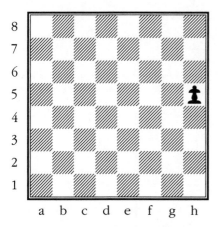

13. What are the key squares for the Black h-pawn?

14. White to move and win.

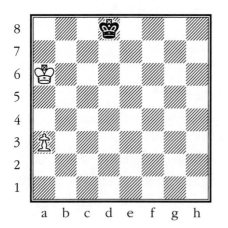

15. White to move and win.

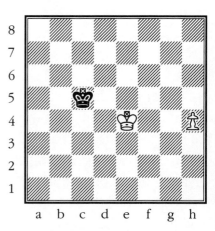

16. Black to move and draw.

Key Squares for Fixed Pawns

Like the rook pawns, fixed (or blocked) Pawns have their own rules for key squares. With fixed Pawns, gaining the key squares will help you win the opposing Pawn, but may not guarantee promotion.

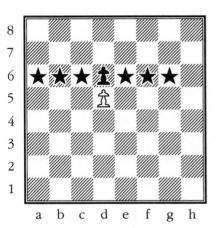

Key squares for fixed pawns are three squares to the side of the opposing pawn.

Once again, we will use the opposition to gain a key square.

1. Ke5   Black has a terrible problem.

If **1. ... Kf7**, White plays **2. Kd6**, winning the Black Pawn, and then pops down to b7 to guard the path of the White Pawn. On the other hand, if

1. ...   **Kd7**
2. Kf6   and White has a key square.

If the theory of key squares is correct—and it is—then White should be able to win the Black Pawn.

On the next page, we will show why the King on the outside key square is so powerful.

Key Squares for Fixed Pawns

With the friendly King on the outside key square, the Pawn and King combine to completely wall out the enemy King.

Now, using the lateral opposition, White will force the enemy King to give up its Pawn.

2.	...	Kc7
3.	Ke7	lateral (side) opposition.
3.	...	Kc8
4.	Kd6	Kb7
5.	Kd7	Black has to lose the Pawn.
5.	...	Kb8
6.	Kxc6	with the winning King position from **Fundamental Position #4**.

There were several other ways Black could have played this, but they all come to the same disastrous end if White plays correctly.

For example, from the diagrammed position:

2.	...	Kd8
3.	Ke6	Kc7

4.	Ke7	Kc8
5.	Kd6	Kb7
6.	Kd7	K any
7.	Kxc6	winning.

While the key squares with blocked Pawns guarantee that the enemy Pawn will be captured, they do not guarantee a winning position. For example, on the next page, we will look at the same position we just examined, but back one rank.

Key Squares for Fixed Pawns

With the White Pawn on rank four (or three or two) instead of rank five, Black draws if the Black King can take the opposition, denying White the crucial key squares.

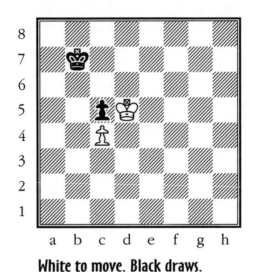

White to move. Black draws.

Here White will capture the Black Pawn, but Black draws the game.

1. Kxc5   Kc7!

Black has the opposition, and thus keeps white from the new key squares. Now that the Pawn on c4 is no longer a fixed or blocked pawn, we have a new situation, and a new set of key squares. The key squares are now on b6, c6, and d6. Since Black has the opposition, White will never get the key squares, and Black can hold the draw.

When a Pawn is blocked, there is one set of key squares. If the blocking Pawn is captured, you have a whole new set of key squares.

If the White Pawn is on the fifth rank, in capturing the Black Pawn, White achieves **Fundamental Position #4** and wins. If the White Pawn is on rank 4, 3, or 2, Black draws by gaining the opposition and denying White the new key squares.

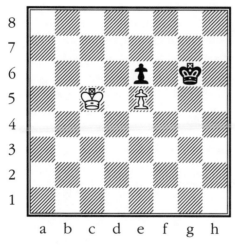

Key Squares for Fixed Pawns

Here both players are about to get a key square (remember, for blocked Pawns the key squares are three squares to the side of the opposing Pawn). Whoever gets there first should have the advantage. If White gets there first, White should win the game, because in capturing the Black Pawn, he achieves **Fundamental Position #4**, which wins every time.

If Black gets there first, he wins the White Pawn, but not the game, because White can take the opposition after the Black King takes the White Pawn, and that will deny Black the key squares needed to promote the Pawn.

However, even getting the key square first, there is a little trick in this position.

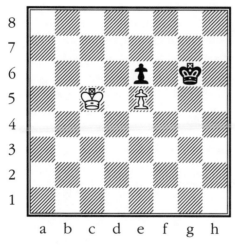

White to move:

1. Kc6   Kg5   Both players have a key square, but White got there first.
2. Kd7!   Not **2. Kd6?**, because Black then plays **2. ... Kf5**, guarding the Black Pawn and attacking the White Pawn, and White has no way to keep the guard on his Pawn on e5, since the Black Pawn attacks d5.

In these positions, you have to attack the enemy Pawn from *below*. Otherwise, you fall into a trap, not only losing the Pawn, but also losing the game, since the White King will be out of position for stopping the Black Pawn from advancing.

   2. ...   Kf5

   3. Kd6   and now it is Black that must abandon his Pawn. Next move, White captures the Black Pawn and easily promotes his own Pawn.

On the next page, we show a variation of this position that has gotten many people in trouble.

Key Squares for Fixed Pawns

Black is already on a key square. Black got there first, so Black should be able to capture the White Pawn.

What should White do? It's a little difficult psychologically to accept the reality that, even though White has the more advanced Pawn, the other side has the advantage. Black's possession of the key square is worth more than the advanced White Pawn. White should play for the draw here. The game should go:

1. Kd4   Kf5 (or Kf4)
2. Kd3   Kxe5
3. Ke3,   taking the opposition and keeping Black from the key squares for his Pawn. As we have seen, with best play from both sides, this position is a draw.

However, if White tries for too much, the draw becomes a loss.

1. Kd6   Kf5!   And White cannot protect the Pawn on e5, and the King can't get back to block the Black Pawn's advance. Black wins.

Another try might be:

1. Kc6   hoping to catch Black in a mistake. If 1. ... Kf5? now, White wins with Kd6. However, Black can win with
1. ...   Kf4!,   coming at the White Pawn from below.
2. Kd6   Kf5   and White will have to abandon his Pawn in a losing position. Black wins.

Key Square Exercises

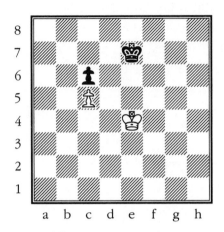

17. White to move and win.

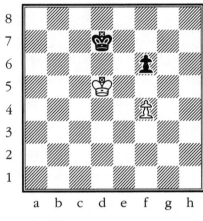

18. White to move and win.

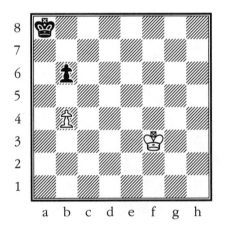

19. White to move and win.

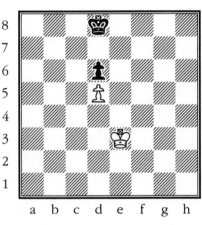

20. White to move and win.

Key Squares for Fixed Pawns

We're going to close this chapter with another challenging puzzle. As before, without looking at the solution below, set this up on a board and try to solve it.

Two against one is usually winning, although there are some interesting drawn positions.

This one, however, is definitely winning if you keep in mind the key squares for blocked Pawns.

1. g3   gives White the blocked pawns and the opposition. If it weren't for the extra Pawn on f2, that would be good for nothing more than a draw, but with the extra Pawn, it's enough to win the game.
1. ...   Kd4
2. f4   gxf, e.p.
3. Kxf3   and White heads for the key square on h5.

Black might also try:

1. ...   Ke5
2. Ke3   taking the direct opposition.
2. ...   Kf5
3. Kd4   with an outflanking maneuver that lands right on the key square for blocked Pawns.

Or:

1. ...   Kf5
2. Kd3   taking the diagonal opposition.
2. ...   Ke5
3. Ke3   converting the diagonal to the direct opposition, and there is no stopping White from getting to a key square.
3. ...   Kf5

4. Kd4   Diagram. That's a key square. The Black Pawn must fall.
4. ...   Kf6   (If **4.** ... Ke6, then White just walks over and picks off the g4-Pawn. If **4.** ... Kg5, then **5.** Ke5 wins one move faster than the main line)
5. Ke4   Kg5
6. Ke5   Kg6
7. Kf4   Kh5
8. Kf5   Kh6
9. Kxg4   and wins.

c h a p t e r 6

Triangulation

There are some endings where the weak side's King is limited by the edge of the board—sometimes there are pawns that similarly limit the King—while the strong side has more space to maneuver in. That extra mobility sometimes gives rise to positions where a special trick called *triangulation* can be used.

The essential idea of triangulation is not difficult. We have seen several endgame situations where having the move is a *disadvantage*. When you have a position that would be winning if the other side had to move, and it is actually your move, you would like to pass and make your opponent move. The rules of chess don't allow a pass, however, so you have to somehow get to the same position with the other side to move.

If you have a position where only the Kings can make meaningful moves, and you can take three moves to get back to the original position, and your opponent must do it in two moves, then you have turned the move over to your opponent.

If you make a triangle to get back to the same spot, while your opponent has to go back and forth between only two squares, you have the same position as before, but with your opponent to move. If your opponent does anything else, you win quickly. If your opponent does what is required, then you still win. If you don't know about *triangulation*, you could wander around making silly moves for a very long time.

Let's look at a typical position calling for *triangulation.*

Triangulation

In our first position, the Black King is limited by the edge of the board. White, on the other hand, has far more space to move around.

If the White King can get to b6, Black's Pawn on a6 will fall.

However, if White goes straight for b6, his first move will be **1. Kc5**. Black then stops White by playing **1. ... Kc7**.

Another idea would be for the White King to get to d6 *after* the Black King moves to d8. Then Black would have to come back to c8, and White would advance the Pawn to the seventh rank without giving check. The Pawn will promote for an easy win.

The problem, as the position stands now, is that White will get to d6 *before* Black goes to d8, and that won't work (try it). Since going directly to c5 or d6 won't work, White has to find something else.

The solution is for White to *triangulate*. That is, White will take three moves to return to d5, while Black will have to return to c8 in only two moves. If Black tries to add a move, there is instant punishment.

Because Black is already on the edge of the board, White has more places to move. Mobility wins. The winning method is

1.	Kc4	Kd8 (if **1. ...** Kc7; **2.** Kc5 wins)
2.	Kd4	Kc8
3.	Kd5	

And now we have exactly the same position, but it is Black's turn to move.

Triangulation

Diagram A

If A)

3.	...	Kd8
4.	Kd6	wins
4.	...	Kc8
5.	c7	Kb7
6.	Kd7	Ka7 (Diagram) laying a trap.
7.	Kc6!	Be careful. Promoting to a Queen now is stalemate.
7.	...	Ka8
8.	c8=Q+	Ka7
9.	Qb7#	

Diagram B

If B)

3.	...	Kc7
4.	Kc5	Kc8
5.	Kb6	Diagram

White has many ways to win from here. No matter what Black does, White simply takes the Pawn on a6, protects his Pawns, and promotes easily. One possible line:

5.	...	Kb8
6.	Kxa6	Kc7
7.	Kb5	Kc8
8.	Kb6	Kb8
9.	c7+	Kc8 White boldly advanced to the seventh with check, knowing that the 'advance with check and your game is a wreck' rule doesn't apply when you have a spare move. The a-Pawn saves the day.
10.	a6!	Kd7
11.	Kb7	K any
12.	c8=Q	and wins.

Triangulation

This situation is very different, in that the edge of the board is not the limiting element in the King's mobility.

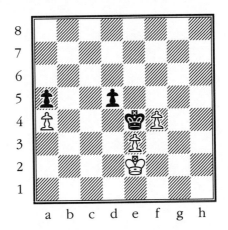

White has the advantage of the protected passed Pawn on f4, but Black's King seems to be holding everything down. Although White is near the edge, it is Black that actually has the more limited of the two Kings. The problem is that Black cannot leave the square of the f4-Pawn. That means it can do no more than toggle back and forth between e4 and f5. Advancing his d-Pawn leads to disaster (**1. ... d4, 2. exd, Kxd4; 3. Kf3** wins for White). If it were Black to move now, there would be nothing but trouble. Backing up to f5 lets the White King advance to d3, and then to d4. From there, the combination of the powerful White King and the strong protected passed Pawn will end the game.

However, it is White to move here. If **1. Kd2**, then the Black Pawn push gets the draw. There would follow **1. ... d4; 2. exd, Kxd4; 3. f5, Ke5; 4. f6, Kxf6, 5. Kc3, Ke6, 6. Kc4,** and Black now has a leisurely stroll down to c8 and over to a8.

White wins by triangulation.

1.	Ke1	Kf5		If	1.	Ke1	d4
2.	Kd2	Ke4			2.	exd4	Kxd4
3.	Ke2				3.	Kf2	Ke4
	Black has no good moves				4.	Kg3	

Triangulation Exercises

White to move and win in all diagrams.

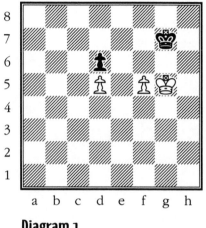

Diagram 1

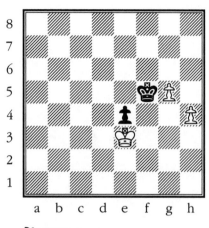

Diagram 2

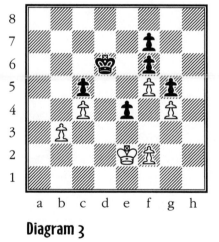

Diagram 3

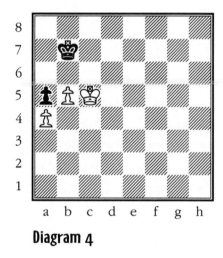

Diagram 4

c h a p t e r

7

The Outside Passed Pawn

An Outside Passed Pawn is a Pawn that is away from the main body of Pawns (it is therefore 'outside' the other Pawns) and cannot be stopped by an enemy Pawn (that makes it a 'passed Pawn').

The value of the outside passed pawn is that it distracts the enemy King from the main gathering of Pawns. The further the Outside Passed Pawn is from the other Pawns, the more dangerous it is. The enemy King will be lured away, so the friendly King can go feast on the enemy Pawns.

In this diagram White has an outside passed Pawn on b5. There are no Black Pawns that can stop this Pawn, and it is far from the Pawns on the other side of the board.

White to play and win.

White's plan is simple and clear. He will abandon the b5-Pawn, forcing the Black King to spend time capturing it. The White King will just stroll over to the kingside and take all the Black Pawns. The Black King will be powerless to stop the marauding White King, because it will have to take time to capture White's outside passed Pawn.

1.	Kc4	Kc7
2.	Kd5	Kb6
3.	Ke5	Kxb5
4.	Kxf5	Kc5
5.	Kxg4	(Diagram next page.)

The Outside Passed Pawn

White sacrificed the outside passed Pawn to reach this position, which is obviously hopeless for Black.

Position after 5. Kxg4

Sometimes the timing is so close that the gain of a single tempo is critical, as in our next example.

In this position, White has to be careful. Just walking over to grab the a5-Pawn won't work. Black has a simple but clever stratagem called Follow the King.

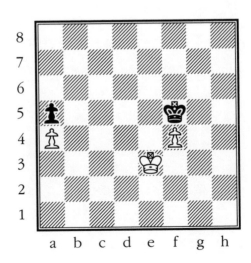

If

1.	Kd4	Kxf4
2.	Kc5	Ke5
3.	Kb5	Kd5
4.	Kxa5	Kc5

Black has the opposition and will eventually either trap the White King on a8 or sneak into the corner himself; either way the game ends in stalemate.

However, White can win by pushing the Black King back a little and gaining time by chasing it further from the Pawn. That way it will take Black two moves to capture the Pawn, not just one as it is now.

1.	Kf3	Kf6
2.	Ke4	Ke6
3.	Kd4	Kf5
4.	Kc5	Kxf4
5.	Kb5	Ke5
6.	Kxa5	Kd6 Black heads for the defensive key square c8.
7.	Kb6 Naturally White doesn't like that idea, and opposes it with the opposition.	
7.	...	Kd7
8.	Kb7 White has a key square for the Rook Pawn, and the next four moves will simply be marching the a-Pawn down for promotion.	

That one extra move White gained by pushing the Black King away from the outside passed Pawn was the necessary step in using the outside passed Pawn correctly. Always calculate.

The Outside Passed Pawn

The outside passed Pawn is a great advantage, but many positions still call for very careful play. For example…

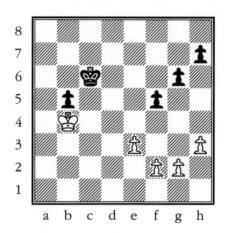

Black to move and win.
Barsov-Brunner, Bern, 1994

The winning idea is to hold back the Black Pawns and to force White to either back up his King or advance his Pawns.

1.	…	Kb6
2.	f3	Kc6
3.	e4	fxe4
4.	fxe4	Kd6!
5.	Kxb5	Ke5
6.	Kc5	Kxe4
7.	Kd6	Kf4
8.	Ke6	Kg3
9.	Kf6	Kxg2
10.	h4	Kg3
11.	Kg5	h5!! wins

In the actual game from the diagram above, Black mistakenly played **1. … h5?**, thereby moving his Pawn base one tempo closer to the White King. It is very easy to misplay these endings. The remaining moves

were: **2.** h4, Kb6; **3.** f3, Kc6; **4.** e4, fxe4; **5.** fxe4, Kb6; **6.** e5, Kc6;
7. e6, Kd6; **8.** Kxb5, Kxe6; **9.** Kc6! (**9.** Kc5? Allows **9.** ... Ke5! -+), **9.** ...
Kf5; **10.** Kd6, Kg4; **11.** Ke6, Kxh4; **12.** Kf6, g5; **13.** Kf5! **(Diagram)** and
Black can't win. If **13.** ... g4; **14.** Kf4, g3; **15.** Kf5! Stalemate.

**Position after 13. Kf5! Even with a Pawn
advantage, Black to play can't win.**

The Outside Passed Pawn Exercises

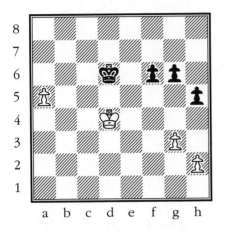

1. White to move and win.

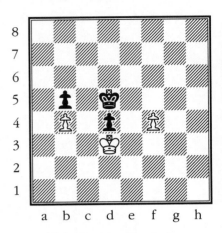

2. White to move and win.

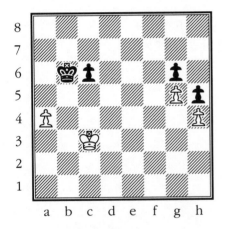

3. White to move.

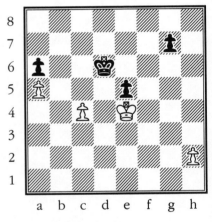

4. White to move

Diagonal March

Because of the geometric design of the chess-board, a direct march of the King along a rank or file is no faster than the seemingly longer distance along the diagonals. This allows the King to go out of his direct path and still not lose time.

For example, how many ways can the White King get from e1 to e8 in seven moves?

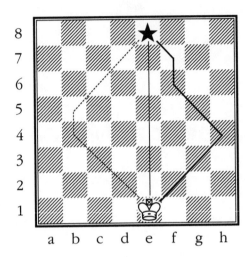

Don't bother counting. There are nearly four hundred ways. Running up the e-file is the most obvious, but the King can also wander out along the diagonal to b4 and b5 and still make it back to e8 in seven moves. It could also go as far afield as h4 and still get to e8 in seven moves.

This ability of the King to use the diagonal gives rise to some surprising King moves in the endings. By moving on a diagonal, the King can actually go in two directions at once.

The following study is something that, even after playing through it hundreds of times, still looks like the work of a magician.

The Diagonal March

8 | 7 | 6 | 5 | 4 | 3 | 2 | 1

a b c d e f g h

1. White to move and draw.
Reti study.

At first view, it seems impossible that White can make a draw here. The White King seems to be hopelessly outside the square of the Black Pawn, and the Black King is only two moves from capturing the White Pawn.

Yet with a diagonal march, the White King can approach both Pawns at once, threatening to protect the White Pawn, and to get in the square of the Black Pawn.

1.	Kg7	h4	or	1.	Kg7	h4			
2.	Kf6	h3		**2.**	Kf6	Kb6			
3.	Ke6	h2		**3.**	Ke5	h3	or	**3.**	...	Kxc6
4.	c7	Kb7		**4.**	Kd6	Draw		**4.**	Kf4	The White
5.	Kd7	h1=Q								King catches the
6.	c8=Q+	Draw.								Pawn and gets
										the draw.

Diagonal March

This is another famous position. If the White King simply heads straight for the Black a-Pawn, the Black King will play Follow the King and, as we saw earlier, imprison the White King on the a-file.

3. White to move and win.
Schlage-Ahues 1921.

It would look like this:

1.	Ke7	Kc3
2.	Kd7	Kd4
3.	Kc7	Kd5
4.	Kb7	Kd6
5.	Kxa7	Kc7	White won't be able to escape. Draw.

Black got the draw because he was able to advance the King on every move.

However, White can use the King more aggressively, defending against the incursion of the Black King.

1.	Ke6	Kc3
2.	Kd5	Kd3
3.	Kc6	Kd4

4. Kb7 Kd5

5. Kxa7 Kc6

6. Kb8 just in time, White takes a key square and has an easy win from here.

By marching forward to slow the enemy King, White did not lose any time in getting to the a7-Pawn, thanks to the wondrous use of the diagonal march. Black, on the other hand had to delay one extra move on the third rank. That one lost tempo cost the game.

Diagonal March

Here are two more delightful uses of the diagonal march for you to figure out.

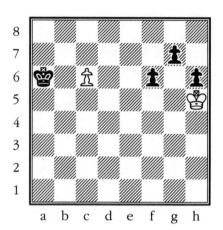

1. White to move and draw.
   This is another Reti marvel.

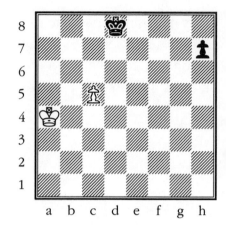

2. White to move and draw.
   From a game by Moravec.

c h a p t e r

9

Mixed Themes in King and Pawn Endings

This chapter is a collection of endings that will challenge your knowledge of the King and Pawn ending. Some are fairly simple, and some are dazzlingly complex.

When you have difficulty, the solution pages will give a pretty complete explanation that should help you understand the ideas posed by the problem.

As an introductory problem, here is one based on a game, Yates-Marshall. (In the actual game, the White Pawn was on f2.)

Black to move and draw.

The Black position looks hopeless. However,

1. ...	Kb2!	Black threatens to advance the a-Pawn, and at the same time, hops on the diagonal leading to h8, where the White Pawn hopes to promote.
2. Kxa4	Kc3	
3. h4	Kd4	and Black is in the square of the Pawn. Draw.

Mixed Themes in King and Pawn Endings

1. White to move and draw.
   Advance with check,
   your game is a wreck . . .

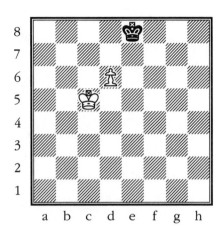

2. White to move and win.
   Black to move and draw.

3. White pushed the Pawn too soon.
Black to move and draw.

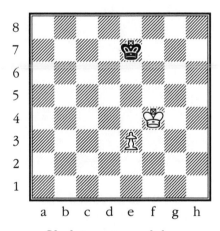

4. Black to move and draw.

King and Pawn Endings

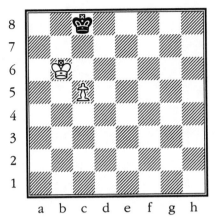

5. White to move and win.

6. White to move and win.

7. White to move and win.

8. White to move and win.

King and Pawn Endings

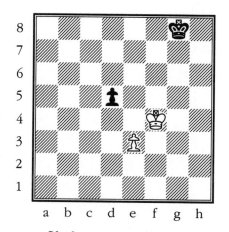

9. Black to move and draw.

10. Black to move and win.

11. White to move and win.

12. White wins no matter who moves.

King and Pawn Endings

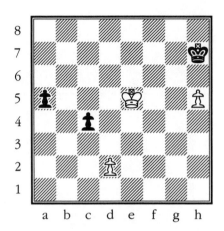

13. Black to move and win.

14. White to move and win.

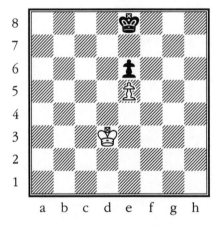

15. White to move and win.

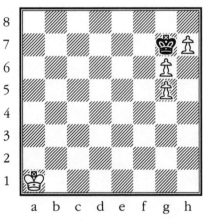

16. White to move and win.

King and Pawn Endings

17. White to move and win *and* Black to move and win.

18. White to move and win.

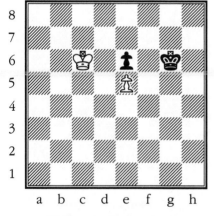

19. White to move and win.

20. White to move. Should White be able to win this?

King and Pawn Endings

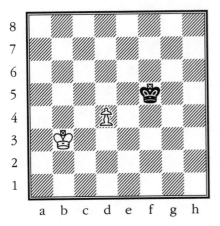

21. Black to move and draw.

22. White to move and draw.

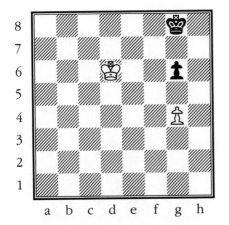

23. White to move and win,
Black to move and draw.

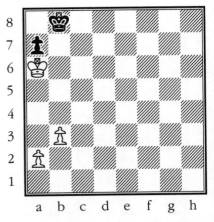

24. White wins. Work out Black
to move *and* White to move.

King and Pawn Endings

25. White to move and win.

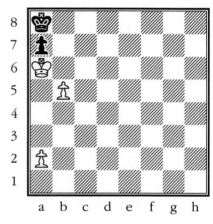

26. White to move and win.

27. White to move and win.

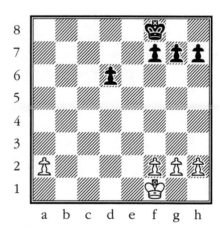

28. White to move and win.

King and Pawn Endings

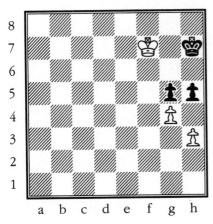

29. White to move and win.

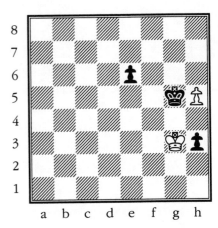

30. White to move and draw.

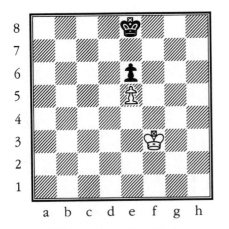

31. White to move and win.

32. White to move and win.

King and Pawn Endings

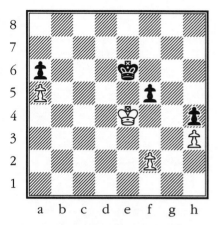

33. White to move and win.

34. White to move and draw.

35. White to move and win.

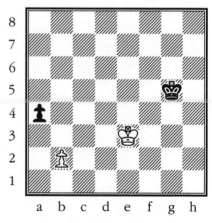

36. White to move and win.

Solutions

Chapter 2: The Square of the Pawn

1. Yes. The square goes from a4 to a8 to e8, up to e4, and back to a4. The Black King on e6 is in the square.
2. White to move and the Pawn promotes because the Black King is not in the square. Black to move: 1. ... Kf6 (or f5 or f7) and the King is in the square. Black will catch the Pawn.
3. No. The King appears to be in the square, but there is a trick to this position. The White Pawn is still on its starting square, so it will go two squares, to a4, on its first move. The King is not in the square, nor can it get in the square as long as the Pawn keeps going forward.
4. Yes. If Black captures the b3-Pawn, he will be out of the square of the a4-Pawn. The White King can easily capture the Black Pawn on h5 and then go over to help his Pawns on the other side of the board.

Practical Applications:

1. This is from Stoltz-Nimzovitch, Berlin, 1927. 1. ... f4!; 2. gxf+, Kd6!; 3. Kd3, g3; 4. Ke2, d3+ (4. ...g2 also works) and Black cruises to an easy win.
2. 1. e4! This secures the draw. Taking on f4 loses because the moving square does not reach the end of the board. A possible continuation after 1. e4 would be 1. ... g3+; 2. fxg, f2; 3. Kg2, fxg, and both Kings are tied to defense, e.g., 4. Kf1, Kc5; 5. Kg2, Kc6; 6. Kf1, Kc5, etc.
3. 1. b4!, cxb; 2. cxb, and now the distance between the Pawns equals the distance to the end of the board. White wins.

Chapter 3: Opposition

1. Kd2 takes the distant opposition.
2. ... Kc5 takes the diagonal opposition.
3. ... Kd8 takes the rectangular opposition. ... Kf8 is also rectangular opposition but is further away. The goal of opposition is to push the enemy King out of the way, so increasing the distance between the Kings is not in the spirit of the opposition.
4. Kc4 takes the direct opposition. Ke4 is diagonal opposition, but the direct is better. The purpose of all the other forms of opposition is to eventually get to the direct opposition. And the purpose of the direct opposition is to push the other King out of the way.
5. 1. Ke5, Ke7 (Black takes the opposition, but he can't hold it.); 2. Kf5. This walks Black off the opposition. He can't get to f7. Now Black plays a little

trick. 2. ... Ke8! (If White plays Kf6, Black gets the opposition back and will be able to stop the Pawn.); 3. Ke6! White doesn't fall for the trick. 3. ... Kf8; 4. Kf6, Kg8; 5. g7, Kh7; 6. Kf7 and the Pawn promotes safely.

6. 1. Kf5, Kf8! Black lays the same trap as in the previous example. 2. Kf6 (the impetuous Ke6 ends in a stalemate: 2. Ke6, Ke8; 3. d7+, Kd8; 4. Kd6 stalemate.); 2. ... Ke8; 3. Ke6, Kd8; 4. d7, Kc7; 5. Ke7 and White promotes next move.

7. 1. Kf4, Kh7; 2. Kg5, Kh8; 3. Kh6! (taking the Pawn throws away the win), 3. ... Kg8; 4. Kxg6, Kf8; 5. f7, Ke7; 6. Kg7 and White promotes next move. If 1. ... g5+; 2. Kf5, g4; 3. Ke6, (don't take the Pawn) g3; 4. f7, Kg7; 5. Ke7, g2; 6. f8=Q+, Kh7; 7. Qf2, g1=Q; 8. Qxg1 winning.

8. 1. Ke6! Black can't hold the opposition. 1. ... Kh7; 2. Kf7, Kh6; 3. Kg8!, Kh5; 4. Kg7, Kxh4; 5. Kxg6, Kg4, 6. f5 and White cruises to a victory.

9. This is similar to #8, but everything is moved over one file. Now that they are not on the edge of the board, Black cannot keep White from getting and holding the opposition. 1. Kh1!, Ke2; 2. Kg2, Ke3; 3. Kg3, Kd3; Kh3! etc. Draw. If 1. ... g4; then 2. Kg2 gets the draw.

10. 1. ... Kb8! With this move, Black walks White off the opposition and secures the draw. All other moves lose. For example, 1. ... Kc7; 2. Kc5, Kb7; 3. Kb5, Kc7; 4. Ka6 winning. After 1. ... Kb8, however, White can make no progress: 1. ... Kb8; 2. Kb5, Kb7 holds the opposition and keeps White from the Key Squares.

11. 1. a8=Q+, Kxa8; 2. Kc6 (*Be Careful: 2. Kc7 is stalemate*) takes the diagonal opposition and wins: 2. ... Kb8; 3. b7, Ka7; 4. Kc7 and White promotes next move. A similar end would occur if the White King had been on a5. Then 2. Ka6 taking the direct opposition would also lead to a win.

12. This famous example of converting distant opposition to direct opposition was given to us by the 3rd World Champion, J. R. Capablanca. 1. Ke2!, taking the distant opposition (same color square on the same rank or file; also, an odd number of squares apart on the same rank, file, or diagonal). 1. ... Ke7 (if 1. ... Kd8; 2. Kf3 wins. If Black then comes back with 2. ... Ke7, White gets back to the opposition with 3. Ke3!). 2. Ke3, Ke6; 3. Ke4 and White has direct opposition. 3. ... Kf6; 4. Kf4, Kg6; 5. Ke5! White pulls an *outflanking maneuver* (see the section on Outflanking). 5. ... Kf7; 6. Kf5, Kg7; 7. Kg5, Kf7; 8. Kxh5, Kf6; 9. Kg4! (don't get boxed in!). Now White heads over to capture the Black b-Pawn, with an easy win.

Chapter 5: Key Squares

1. b4, c4, and d4.
2. b5, c5, and d5.
3. b6, c6, and d6.
4. b6, c6, and d6, and b7, c7 and d7.

5. c3! White to move means Black has the opposition. Now we see why the key squares leave an empty square between the King and Pawn. If Black has the opposition, that empty square allows White to throw the move back to Black, giving White the opposition. It is true that in moving forward, White pushed the key squares up to b5, c5, and d5, but since White has the opposition, he will get a new key square whichever way Black moves. For example, after 1. ... Kb6; 2. Kd5 and White occupies a key square.

6. Kc5! This keeps the key squares and also takes the opposition so the King can advance to the next level of key squares. White should win this position. Pushing the Pawn throws the key squares up to the sixth rank, and gives Black the opposition and the draw. *Pushing the Pawn too soon is a typical mistake in these positions.*

7. Kc5! This takes the opposition to get a key square on the sixth rank next move. White should win easily. (Note that pushing the Pawn with 1. c5, throws away the win. That allows Black to block White by gaining the opposition with 1. ... Kd7. If that happens, White can't get a key square and the game should end in a draw.)

8. Kc6! Again, pushing the Pawn will not win. White is on a key square, so there must be a way to win. There is: by getting in front of the Pawn and taking the opposition, achieving Fundamental Position #4, White forces Black out of the way. When Black moves to either side, White simply guards the path on the other side. For example: 1. Kc6, Kb8; 2. Kc7 and the Pawn walks in to promotion.

9. The key squares are b5, c5, and d5. White can easily get to them. The best key square is always the one on the same file as the Pawn. White plays either 1. Kc4 or 1. Kd4, aiming for c5. *Pushing the Pawn is a mistake.* 1. c4 pushes the key squares up to the sixth rank, and gives Black the opposition. 1. ... Kd7; 2. Kd4, Kd6; and this should be a draw. Play out this position many times until you are completely familiar with all the variations.

10. Again, we begin by identifying the key squares: here they are f6, g6, and h6. Black is very close to f6, so the direct path is not going to work. 1. Kf2 wins. 1. ... Kd7; 2. Kg3! White is heading for the outside key square. 2. ... Ke6; 3. Kh4, Kf6; 4. Kh5, Kg7; 5. Kg5, Kf7; 6. Kh6 and White achieves the goal of occupying a key square.

11. In this position, key squares are a5, b5, and c5. Clearly, c5 is very close to the Black King. Therefore, it only makes sense to go toward a5. So the first move is 1. Kb2! (Heading straight up won't work: 1. Kc2, Kd7; 2. Kc3, Kc7! With the distant opposition, Black will now be able to stop the Pawn from promoting. For example, 3. Kb4, Kb6; 4. Kc4, Kc6; 5. b4, Kb6; 6. b5, Kb7; 7. Kc5, Kc7; 8. b6+, Kb7; 9. Kb5, Kb8; 10. Kc6, Kc8; 11. b7+, Kb8; 12. Kb6 stalemate.) 1. ... Kd7; 2. Ka3, Kc6; 3. Ka4, grabbing the diagonal opposition.

3. ... Kb6; 4. Kb4, turning the diagonal into the direct opposition. 4. ... Kc6; 5. Ka5, and White has taken a key square. Play might continue: 5. ... Kb7; 6. Kb5, Kc7; 7. Ka6, Kb8; 8. Kb6, Ka8; 9. b4, Kb8; 10. b5, Ka8; 11. Kc7 and wins.

12. Here again, we have to be careful. Going under the Pawn is the answer: 1. Kf2, and circle around behind as in diagrams 10 and 11 above.

13. g1 and g2.

14. 1. Kg6 taking the opposition as it heads for the key square g7. 1. ... Ke7; 2. Kg7 and wins.

15. 1. Kb7 takes the key square. White simply marches the Pawn down to a8.

16. 1. ... Kd6; 2. Kf5, Ke7; 3. Kg6, Kf8 and Black has the defensive key square. White will not promote.

17. 1. Ke5. White gains the opposition. 1. ... Kd7. Black has to keep the White King from d7, but that allows White to claim the outside key square. 2. Kf6! and wins.

18. 1. f5! With this move, White fixes the Pawns, and automatically gains the opposition. Black will have to let White in to the outside key square c6. 1. ... Ke7; 2. Kc6!

19. 1. b5. Again, White fixes the Pawns. The next step is to get to a key square. 1. ... Kb7; 2. Ke4, Kc7; 3. Ke5! (not 3. Kd5, allowing Black to get the opposition with 3. ...Kd7), Kd7; 4. Kd5 now White has the opposition, and will use that to get a key square.

20. Here again, the battle is over the key squares. 1. Kf4, Ke7; 2. Kg5, Kf7; 3. Kf5, Ke7; 4. Kg6.

Chapter 6: Triangulation

1. 1. f6+! The trick is to push the Black King back so he runs out of room to maneuver.1. ...Kf8; 2. Kf4, Kg8; 3. Kg4, Kf8; 4. Kg5 and Black is in zugzwang. If 4. ...Kg8; 5. Kg6, Kf8; 6. f7, Ke7; 7. Kg7 wins. If 4. ... Kf7; 5. Kf5, Kf8; 6. Ke6 wins.

2. Black cannot move the King down to the fourth rank or it will be outside the square of the g-Pawn. Also, if the King ventures over to the e-file, White advances the h-Pawn. That means it must shuttle back and forth between g6 and f5. Anytime White is on e3, Black must be on f5 to guard the Pawn. White has two squares to maneuver on (e2 and f2), while Black has only one. With this in mind, the solution is simple. 1. Ke2 (or Kf2), Kg6; 2. Kf2, Kf5; 3. Ke3, Ke5; 4. h5! Kf5; 5. h6 (or 5. g6) and Black has no way to both stop the Pawns and guard his own e-Pawn.

3. In this puzzle, Black has to get to e5 to guard the e-Pawn *after* White moves to e3. Unfortunately for Black, there is only one square available to get to e5,

and he is on it right now. A little delaying move by White undoes Black. 1. Kd2! Ke5; 2. Ke3 and Black must abandon the Pawn. White wins the Pawn, then produces a passed Pawn on the Queenside and wins the game. 2. ... Kc6; 3. Kd3, Kb7 rectangular opposition; 4. Kc2, Ka6; 5. Kb2, Kb6; 6. Ka3, Ka5; 7. b4+!, cb+; 8. Kb3, Kb6; 9. Kxb4, Kc6; 10. c5, Kc7; 11. Kb5, Kb7; 12. c6+, Kc7; 13. Kc5, Kc8; 14. Kd6, Kd8; 15. c7+, Kc8; 16. Ke7 and White takes all the Black Pawns.

4. Every Black move here loses. 1. ... Kc7; 2. b6+, Kb7; 3. Kb5 is an easy win. 1. ... Ka7; 2. Kc6, followed by Kb6 and Kxa5 wins. The problem is that it is White's turn. Pushing the Pawn now won't work: 1. b6, Ka6! and Black gets a draw: 2. Kc6 stalemate, and 2. b7, Kxb7 is a draw because Black can park his King in the corner and relax. White must triangulate to give Black the move in this position. However, before triangulating, White has to pull another trick. First, give Black the opposition, then take it away. At that point, White will be in position to triangulate. 1. Kd6, Kb6; Black has the opposition. White must get it back. 2. Ke6, Kc7; 3. Kd5, Kb6; 4. Kd6 and White has triangulated to get the opposition. 4. ... Kb7; 5. Kc5. White has achieved the goal.

Chapter 7: The Outside Passed Pawn

1. 1. a6, Kc6; 2. a7, Kb7; 3. Kd5, h4; 4. Ke6! (accepting doubled h-Pawns would lead to a draw after 4. gxh4, f5!) 4. ... hxg3; 5. hxg3, f5; 6. Kf6 and Black has no good moves. The White a-Pawn distracted the Black King, leaving the Kingside Pawns with no protector.

2. 1. f5, Ke5; 2. f6, Kxf6; 3. Kxd4, Ke6; 4. Kc5, Kd7; 5. Kxb5, Kc7; 6. Ka6 White is on a key square and wins easily.

3. 1. Kc4, c5; 2. a5+, Kxa5; 3. Kxc5, Ka4; 4. Kd6, Kb4; 5. Ke6, Kc5; 6. Kf6, Kd6; 7. Kxg6 and the position is clearly hopeless for Black.

4. This one is very tricky. The right move is 1. h4! bringing the h-Pawn closer to promotion. In this case, the outside passed Pawn is a little deceptive; it is the White c-Pawn. However, we want to get the position of the Pawn we want to promote as strong as possible before we try distracting the enemy King. 1. ... Kc5; 2. Kxe5, Kxc4; 3. Kf5, Kb4; 4. Kg6, Kxa5; 5. Kxg7, Kb4; 6. Kg6, a5; 7. h5, a4; 8. h6, a3; 9. h7, a2; 10. h8 = Q and wins, since the White Queen controls Black's promotion square.

Chapter 8: Diagonal March

1. This is another study by Reti. We will give three variations. 1. Kg6!, Kb6; 2. Kxg7, f5; 3. Kf6, f4; 4. Ke5, f3; 5. Kd6 and both Pawns will promote. Even with the extra Pawn, Black has nothing better than a draw. Running with the f-Pawn immediately is also a draw: 1. Kg6, f5; 2. Kxg7!, f4; 3. Kf6, f3; 4. Ke7!

f2; 5. c7, Kb7; 6. Kd7, f1=Q; 7. c8=Q+, again, with a draw. Similarly, running with the h-Pawn is a draw: 1. Kg6, h5; 2. Kxg7, h4; 3. Kxf6, h3; 4. Ke7, Kb6 (4. ...h2; 5. c7 draws); 5. Kd7, h2; 6. c7, h1=Q; 7. c8=Q+ draw.

2. White gets the draw by faking a run at his own promotion. 1. Kb5, h5; 2. Kc6 with the very real threat of 3. Kb7 and both sides promote. 2. ... Kc8; 3. Kd5 and by means of a diagonal march, White has managed to get in the square of the h-Pawn.

K&P Mixed Themes

1. 1. d7+. Advance with check and your game is a wreck. 1. ... Kd8; 2. Kd6 stalemate. White can't win this if Black plays well. Best is for White to give Black a chance to make a mistake: 1. Kd5, Kd7; 2. Ke5, Ke8?? (2. ... Kd8 keeps the draw); 3. Ke6 and White sneaks into a win. As a matter of courtesy, at the elementary school level, if your opponent plays accurately for a couple of moves, accept the draw. Higher levels take the draw sooner.

2. 1. Kc6 diagonal opposition. 1. ... Kd8; 2. d7. Advance to the seventh rank *without* giving check and you win. Black to move is a draw. The clearest is to just immediately play 1. ... Kd7. 1. ... Kd8 is also a draw.

3. 1. ... Kh8! secures the draw. If 2. g7+, Kg8; 3. Kg6 stalemate. 2. Kf7 is also stalemate. Finally, 2. Kg5 (or 2. Kf5) allows Black to get in front of the Pawn with 2. ... Kg7 and another drawn ending results.

4. 1. ... Kf6 takes the opposition and keeps White from getting a key square.

5. 1. Kc6 is our famous winning position. Now 1. ... Kd8; 2. Kb7, guarding the path of the Pawn all the way to promotion.

6. 1. Kf7, Kh8; 2. Kg6, Kg8; 3. Kh6, Kh8; 4. g6, Kg8; 5. g7, Kf7; 6. Kh7 wins.

7. 1. Kg4, Kg7; 2. Kg5, Kh8; 3. Kf5 (not 3. Kf6?? Stalemate), Kg7; 4. h8=Q+, Kxh8; 5. Kf6, Kg8; 6. g7, Kh7; 7. Kf7 wins.

8. 1. Kd7 (opposition) 1. ... Kb6; 2. Kc8! (outflanking), 2. ... Kb5; 3. Kc7, Kxb4; 5. Kxc6, Kc4; 6. d5 winning.

9. 1. ... d4! 2. exd (not taking doesn't work) now the key squares are c6, d6, and e6. 2. ... Kf8! taking the distant opposition to keep the White King off the key squares. 3. Ke5, Ke7 draws.

10. 1. ... a5! wins for Black. The barrier is up on b5 and b4, and if White's King takes on c6, it will be out of the square of the a-Pawn.

11. The battle is over the key squares. White is aiming for c6, d6, or e6. Black must keep White off those squares. 1. Kc3, Kb7; 2. Kd4, Kc7; 3. Ke5! diagonal opposition. (Not 3. Kd5? Kd7!). 3. ... Kd7; 4. Kd5, Kc7; 5. Ke6 White has a key square. 5. ... Kb7; 6. Kd7, Kb8; 7. Kc6, Ka7; 8. Kc7, Ka8; 9 Kxb6 winning.

12. White to move:1. Ke6, Kc8; 2. c7, Kxc7; 3. Ke7 wins as in #11. Black to move: 1. ... Kc8; 2. c7!, Kxc7; 3. Ke6 wins. Black can also set some stale-

mate traps: 1. ... Kd8, 2. c7+, Kc8! 3. Kd6 (3. Kc6? is stalemate), Kb7; 4. Kd7, Ka7! 5. Kc6 (5. c8=Q or 5. c8=R are both stalemate), Ka8; 6. c8=Q+, Ka7; 7. Qb7#.

13. This is a battle about the square of the Pawn. 1. ... c3!; 2. dxc3 (forced), a4; and now that Black has clogged up the diagonal, even though the White King is in the square, it cannot catch the Pawn.

14. Similar to #10. 1. h4 gets the win.

15. 1. Kc4! (rectangular opposition), Kd7, 2. Kb5 (diagonal opposition), Kc7; 3. Kc5 (direct opposition), Kd7; 4. Kb6 (key square and wins). Black might also try, after 1. Kc4, Kf7, 2. Kc5, Kg6; 3. Kc6! (Black was hoping White would make a mistake with 3. Kd6?, allowing 3. ... Kf5! and wins.) 3. ... Kg5 (still hoping for 4. Kd6?) 4. Kd7! and wins.

16. 1. Kb2, Kh8; 2. Kc3, Kg7; 3. Kd4, Kh8; 4. Ke5, Kg7; 5. h8=Q+, Kxh8; 6. Kf6, Kg8; 7. g7, Kh7; 8. g8=Q+, Kxg8; 9. Kg6 winning.

17. White to move: 1. Kd7 (careful—1. Kd6 loses to Kf5!), Kf5; 2. Kd6 and Black is in zugzwang. Black to move: 1. ... Kf4; 2. Kd6, Kf5 wins.

18. 1. Kb6!

19. 1. Kd7!

20. No. If 1. Kd6, Kf5! Wins for Black. 1. Kc6, Kf4!; 2. Kd6, Kf5 wins for Black. 1. Kc4, Kf4; 2. Kd4, Kf5 wins the Pawn, but the game is a draw. Finally, 1. Kd4, Kf4 also gets the Pawn but again, the game is a draw.

21. 1. ... Ke6!; 2. Kc4, Kd6 draw.

22. 1. Kb4, h4; 2. Kc5, h3; 3. Kd6 gets the draw. If 1. ... Kb6; 2. Kc4, Kxc6; 3. Kd4 puts the White King in the square of the Pawn. Draw. Finally, 1. Kb4, Kb6; 2. Kc4, h4; 3. Kd5, Kc7; 4. Ke4 draw. And 3. ... h3; 4. Kd6, h2; 5. c7, Kb7; 6. Kd7, h1=Q; 7. c8=Q+ draw.

23. White to move: You need to think key squares to get this one. Think of blocked Pawns. What are the key squares for blocked Pawns? Three squares out to the side of the enemy Pawn. All White has to do is advance the Pawn and his King is already on a key square. So: 1. g5! If 1. ... Kg7; then 2. Ke7 takes the opposition and gets the win. If 1. ... Kf7; then 2. Kd7 takes the opposition and gets the win.

Black to move: 1. ... g5! With best play, Black will lose the Pawn but get the opposition, keeping White from getting to a key square. For example, 1. ... g5; 2. Ke6, Kg7; 3. Kf5, Kf7; 4. Kxg5, Kg7. Once the Pawn is captured, the new key squares are f6, g6, and h6. Black has the opposition, so the draw is assured.

24. We need to look way into the future to figure this out. It all comes down to the question of advancing to the seventh without giving check. White has the ability to advance the a-Pawn one or two squares. That means White can control when to make a protected advance to b6. White wants the position in this diagram with White to move. Now 1. b6 leaves Black helpless. Taking the Pawn gives White the win: 1. ... axb6; 2. axb6, Kb8; 3. b7, Kc7; Ka7 and wins. *Not* taking also gives White the win: 1. ... Kb8; b7 (advancing to the seventh rank without giving check), 3. Kc7; 4. Kxa7 winning.

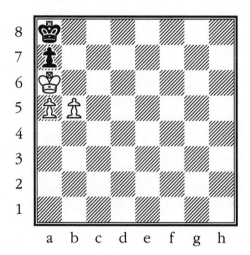

The question is, how do we get to this analysis diagram from the situation in #20? Some calculation reveals that with White to move, the Pawn needs to stop at a3, whereas with Black to move, the a-Pawn must advance two squares on the first move. Exact calculation is needed here, and fortunately, exact calculation is possible because Black can do nothing but toggle back and forth between a8 and b8 with the King. So we can see that after five full moves, Black will be on a8. With White moving first, we have two moves of the b-Pawn and we need three moves of the a-Pawn. That will only happen if the a-Pawn goes one square at a time up to a5.

Now let's make it Black to move. White needs to get to our analysis position one move sooner, which is easily done by simply moving the a-Pawn to a4 in one move instead of two.

25. 1. Kd4, Kh8; 2. Ke5, Kg7; 3. h8=Q+ Kxh8; 4. Kf6, Kg8; 5. g7, Kh7; 6. Kf7, Kh6; 7. g8=Q wins.

26. If you didn't get #24, this is another chance at the same idea. The winning idea is the same. You want to be able to advance to the seventh rank without giving check. 1. a4, Kb8; 2. a5, Ka8; 3. b6, axb6; 4, axb6, Kb8; 5. b7, Kc7; 6. Ka7 wins. If it were Black to move, White would only go to a3 on the first Pawn move.

27. This is a problem about spare moves. First we stalemate the Black King so Black will have to move the Pawn. Then we free the King. If the King moves, White gets a clear win. If Black pushes the Pawn, White blocks it and waits for Black to move the King off the promotion square. 1. Kf6, h6; 2. Kg6, h5; 3. h4, Ke7; 4. Kg7 wins. If Black plays 1. ... h5; 2. h3! (2. h4 is stalemate.)

28. Another outside passed Pawn. The winning idea here is to distract the Black King with the outside passed Pawn, and then while the King is away on the queenside, run over and take the Black Pawns on the Kingside. Possible moves might be: 1. Ke2, Ke7; 2. Kd3, Kd7; 3. Kd4, Kc6; 4. Kc4 Black is out of useful moves. 4. ... h6; 5. a4, h5; 6. a5, g6; 7. a6, Kb6; 8. Kd5, Kxa6; 9. Kxd6, Kb5; 10. Ke7, f5; 11. Kf6, f4; 12. Kxg6, h4; 13. Kg5, h3; 14. g3, fxg3; 15. fxg3, Kc5; 16. Kg4 and 17. Kxh3.

29. 1. h4! The idea is to get a g-Pawn marching up the file. There is no way for Black to stop this. If 1. ... hxg4, then 2. hxg5 wins. Even though Black has the move, White gets it back when he checks the Black King. For example, 2. ... g3; 3. g6+, Kh6, 4. g7 wins. The alternative capture, 1. ... gxh4, allows 2. g5! h3; 3. g6+ Kh6; 4. g7, h2; 5. g8=Q, 6. h1=Q, Qg6#.

30. This one is all about key squares and the opposition. 1. Kh2!, Kxh5; 2. Kxh3, Kg5; 3. Kg3, Kf5; 4. Kf3, Ke5; 5. Ke3. White has the opposition, so Black cannot get to the key squares. If White goofs and takes the Pawn, Black wins: 1. Kxh3, Kxh5 Black has the opposition; 2. Kg3, Kg5; 3. Kf3, Kf5; 4. Ke3, Ke5; 5. Kd3, Kf4! Black has a key square and should win easily.

31. 1. Kg4!, Kf7; 2. Kh5 and wins. E.g., 2. ... Kg7; 3. Kg5, Kf7; 4. Kh6 gets the outside key square.

32. The obvious 1. Kd5 won't work. The Black King slips around *behind* the White King and comes at the White Pawn while the White King goes after the Black Pawn. Black can get the draw. Work this out for yourself. The right move is 1. Kd4! Kc6; 2. Ke5, Kc5; 3. f4! wins. If 1. ... Kb4, 2. f4 wins.

33. This is a problem about who has the extra move. 1. Kf4, Kf6; 2. f3! Black has to move the King. He has no spare Pawn moves to make. Since the King has no good moves, Black is lost. 2. ... Kg6; 3. Ke5, Kg5; 4. f4+, Kg6; 5. Ke6 and the Black f-Pawn falls.

34. Trying for a win actually loses. For example, 1. Kc4, Kf4; 2. Kb5, Ke4; 3. Kc6, Ke5 and Black wins. The right idea is to be satisfied with the draw. 1. Ke3, Kf5; 2. Kf3 (opposition), Ke5; 3. Ke3, Kxd5, Kd3 draw.

35. 1. Kd4! Nothing else works. 1. ... Ke6; 2. Kc5, Ke7; 3. Kd5, Kd7; 4. Ke5, Ke7; 5. g5! At just the right moment White creates blocked Pawns and gives himself the opposition. 5. ... Kf7; 6. Kd6! White has a key square and wins.

36. Black's plan is to advance his a-Pawn, forcing White to capture. White will then have an a-Pawn. If Black can then get down to c8 with the King, White will not get the key squares and Black can get the draw. White's solution is to block out the Black King and at the same time approach the Pawns. The diagonal march does the trick. 1. Kd4! Kf5; 2. Kc5! and wins. If 2. ... a3; 3. bxa3, and White can easily get to the key square b7. If 2. ... Ke6 or 2. ... Ke5; 3. Kb4 squashes all hope. After 3. ... a3; 4. Kxa3 is an easy win.